TINY
HISTORIES

DIXE WILLS

TINY
HISTORIES

Trivial events & trifling
decisions that changed
British history

Hardie Grant

QUADRILLE

Publishing director: Sarah Lavelle
Creative director: Helen Lewis
Commissioning editor: Céline Hughes
Cover designer: Nathan Burton
Designer: Emily Lapworth
Production director: Vincent Smith
Production controller: Tom Moore

This edition published in 2019 by Quadrille,
an imprint of Hardie Grant Publishing

Quadrille
52–54 Southwark Street
London SE1 1UN
quadrille.co.uk

ISBN: 978 178713 459 1

Printed in China

Pour O

'Le cœur a ses raisons,
que la raison ne connaît point.'

Contents

Science

Politics

Music & Literature

Health & Safety

Introduction

It might be difficult to believe when reading the news but the Britain we live in is not entirely shaped by the whim of the government and the decisions of ministers blessed with varying degrees of wisdom, but very often by tiny, apparently insignificant events. The wars the nation has fought, the great advances made in science, the food we eat, the music we listen to and the politics that shape our daily life – all of these have been governed to a certain extent by incidents or events that may have appeared completely inconsequential at the time.

For example, there's the split-second decision that could just as easily have gone another way, with completely different consequences; the small gesture of defiance carried out by an ordinary man or woman that sparked a movement or even a revolution; the chance meeting of two people whose subsequent work together far exceeded the sum of its parts; the moment of carelessness that resulted in a catastrophic defeat or disaster or, alternatively, brought about some extraordinary discovery that would not otherwise have been made; or the idea nurtured in obscurity that blossomed into something astonishing.

In *Tiny Histories* we go behind the scenes to look upon a host of fascinating and extraordinary stories of seemingly trivial events that have had enormous repercussions, in many cases moulding both the society we live in today and the people we are. It's a surprisingly little-known fact, for example, that we owe the existence of the greatest scientific manual ever written to a wager in a coffee house that didn't even involve the book's author. The signing of the document that laid out for the first time the rights and freedoms that all Britons should enjoy came about as a consequence of a previous king's fatal desire to eat a large number of an eel-like fish. Much of British politics in the 1960s and '70s was determined by the shifting in the schedules of a television show, and an interview on a sports programme. The reason why it's easier to make jokes in English rather than in German is all down to a disastrous decision taken by an obscure local leader in Essex in 991. Meanwhile, science fiction was invented because a duchess liked to tag on little extras to the books she wrote on natural philosophy.

I should perhaps emphasise that this is not a book of 'what ifs' – those speculations on what might have happened if only some event had turned out differently (yes, OK, we get it – had Hitler conquered Britain, life would have been a bit rubbish). The examples contained within these pages are arguably even more extraordinary than their counter-factual cousins because we can see for ourselves what effect they've had on the nation (and often the world beyond) without indulging in a moment's conjecture.

Finally, I hope that the events in *Tiny Histories* are an inspiration to us all. If nothing else, they show that any one of us – however insignificant we may feel – may yet come to have an impact on the world that is far greater than we might possibly imagine.

Dixé Wills

War

Famously decried by Motown soul singer Edwin Starr as being good for 'absolutely nothing', war has nonetheless proved itself a disturbingly easy state for the British to get into. The vicissitudes of armed conflict also make it a rich breeding ground for the sort of trivial occurrence whose repercussions are amplified and so go on to echo down the ages.

Ealdor Byrhtnoth carries out a misguided act of chivalry

Walk across the short but well-defined causeway to Northey Island and you're travelling over a strip of land that has arguably had a greater and longer-lasting impact on the history of Britain than almost any other portion of the nation. Furthermore, the ill-advised act of chivalry that took place here has few rivals when it comes to the magnitude and scope of the consequences it produced. Not only did it result in one of the most extortionate and prolonged cases of blackmail the world has ever seen, but it determined who ruled the nation 75 years later, the very language that Britons would speak, and even had an impact on their ability to tell jokes.

None of this, however, could be guessed at on arriving at the scene today. Less than two miles away from the fishermen's cottages and weatherboarded terraces of Maldon in Essex, Northey Island is a low, marshy, unprepossessing place speckled with trees. Its narrow causeway – probably built by the Romans – is just a few hundred yards long, threading itself out across marshland and then over the deep black mud of the river bed which, when the sun and tide are both out, shines like molten jet. It is the slenderness of this causeway that played a significant part in the events that unravelled there.

It was in the year 991 that a fleet of 93 ships led by the Norwegian Olaf Tryggvason sailed up the River Blackwater and landed on the 300-acre Northey Island, apparently having mistaken it for the mainland in the mist. Warned of the invasion, a small militia was hastily assembled by a Saxon ealdor (local leader) called Byrhtnoth. When the murk eventually cleared, Tryggvason shouted over that he and his horde would go away if they were given gold, an offer the 60-year-old ealdor rejected. Both sides then patiently waited for the tide to go out so that they could settle the matter by force of arms. Not having read their 'Horatio at the Bridge', the Vikings were surprised to find that the extreme narrowness of the causeway meant that a mere three of Byrhtnoth's soldiers – Wulfstan, Aelfere and Maccus – were able to hold back their 3,000-strong army. Or so goes the tale at least. In reality, one imagines that all of Byrhtnoth's small force was employed in keeping the Norsemen bottled up on the island.

Tryggvason soon tired of this and complained to Byrhtnoth that having his troops cooped up in this manner was not playing the game. The Saxon ealdor, chivalrous to a fault, agreed. He fatally allowed the Vikings to come across the causeway unmolested so that the opposing forces might fight on equal terms on an adjacent field. In doing this, he somehow overlooked the fact that his band of peasant warriors was rather seriously outnumbered. The Vikings thanked their hosts, before taking great care to butcher them almost to a man. According to an epic poem about the battle written four years later by an anonymous hand, Byrhtnoth himself was killed in the mêlée, pierced by a poisoned Viking spear before being hacked to pieces.

So began that inglorious chapter of Anglo-Saxon history that saw the country bled dry by the payment of the so-called Danegeld – the Danes having taken note of how easy it was for their Norwegian brethren to exact money from the English. Naturally enough, each time the hapless king – take a bow, Æthelred II (the Unready) – paid the Danes off with boatloads of money (the initial payment in 991 was an eye-watering 3,300kg of silver), he found that they returned not long afterwards to ask for more. Then the Swedes got in on the act and proved themselves even more adroit at it. Such was the success of these extortion rackets that archaeologists have excavated far more English coinage from this period in Scandinavia than they have in England. It's estimated that in total the Anglo-Saxons gave over more than six million silver coins, collectively weighing in at over 100 tonnes.

However, it needn't have been that way at all. Had Byrhtnoth simply kept Tryggvason's forces on Northey Island until an army large enough to defeat it had been assembled, England would not have needed to buy its way out of trouble. As a result, the nation would almost certainly not have found itself visited seventy-five years later by Harald Hardrada. The Norwegian thought to go one better than his Nordic countrymen and cousins: rather than merely extort money out of the English – who were understandably seen throughout Scandinavia as a soft touch – he aspired to their throne.

Had Hardrada not landed his army on the Yorkshire coast in 1066, King Harold II of England would not have had to march his soldiers at full speed from London to defeat the invaders at Stamford Bridge on 25 September. Consequently, the Saxon king's army would not have been so exhausted and depleted in numbers when, just 19 days and a heroic 240-mile southward march later, it had to face William, the Duke of Normandy's troops near Hastings. Since, even under these circumstances, Harold's forces came close to winning the battle, it's not stretching credibility to claim that had they been at full strength – both physically and numerically – they would indeed have done so.

William was crowned king of England at Westminster Abbey on Christmas Day 1066. In an eerie echo of the events of 991, on his way to claim the throne he, too, had found his army held back (albeit temporarily) by a much smaller force: on this occasion one defending London Bridge. Once crowned, he swiftly set about the Normanisation of his new territory. This included the introduction of Norman French as the official tongue. Thus the English language experienced a great sea change as its Germanic Saxon words started to be eased out in favour of the more sensuous-sounding Norman French vocabulary. Thus, for example, when an English speaker today wishes to get across the idea that something is bendy, they will say that it is 'malleable' or 'pliable' rather than that it is 'schwank', as might be the case if Byrhtnoth (and thus Harold) had won. Many may say that that is no bad thing.

Furthermore, the change in language meant that rather than habitually ending sentences with a verb (as is the case with German today), the English are more likely to finish them with a noun or an adjective. Since there are far more nouns and adjectives than there are verbs, this makes it much easier to tell the sort of joke known as a 'switch'. This works by substituting the word the hearer is expecting at the end of a sentence for one that changes the entire meaning of it. As a result, being funny in English is arguably less challenging than it is in German. This is a good thing to keep in mind next time you hear someone ribbing the Germans for their apparent lack of humour.

And all this occurred simply because of a single rash decision made by an obscure local leader on the banks of a minor Essex river over a thousand years ago.

A sailor has an ear cut off (and possibly pickled)

Countless are the atrocities committed in wartime. It is a much rarer occurrence, however, for a relatively minor act of barbarity to galvanise a nation into declaring war. And yet that is precisely what occurred in the case of the curiously named War of Jenkins' Ear, a conflict that lasted almost a decade. During that time it merged seamlessly with the War of the Austrian Succession and was notable for the two firsts it created in military history, both of which paved the way for yet more anguish and suffering to be heaped upon future generations.

The incident that helped spark this off cannot have seemed like a minor act of barbarity to the man on whom it was inflicted. Robert Jenkins, the Welshman whose ear was to become famous, captained a brig called *Rebecca* which, in the spring of 1731, was cruising the Caribbean, where he was engaged in a little light smuggling. Under the terms of the Treaty of Utrecht of 1713, Spain had granted Britain a 30-year *asiento* – the right to supply the Spanish colonies of the New World with a limitless number of slaves and up to 500 tonnes of produce per annum. Naturally, the temptation to get around the latter quota proved too much for some, and undeclared goods often found their way to the colonists. Accordingly, as a concession to Spain in the 1729 Treaty of Seville, Britain afforded the Spanish the right to waylay British ships to ensure that they were trading within the restrictions laid down by the *asiento*.

So it came to pass that on 9 April 1731, Juan de León Fandiño, the captain of a Spanish patrol vessel called *La Isabela*, spotted the two-masted squared-rigged *Rebecca* and decided to find out what she was up to. *La Isabela* was brought up alongside the brig and Fandiño and other officers boarded her. What happened next was to have repercussions that would resonate down the centuries. According to reports, Jenkins was accused by the Spaniards of smuggling and was tied to a mast, at which point Fandiño (or possibly an officer named Dorce) drew out a cutlass and hacked at Jenkins' left ear. Another member of the boarding party stepped forward and tore off the dangling appendage. Fandiño is then reputed to have proclaimed something along the lines of: 'Go! And tell your king that I will do the same to him if he dares to do what you have done.' The coast guards then assaulted the crew, plundered the ship and set it adrift without navigational instruments, an act that might well have sent them to their doom. Two months later, however, the *Rebecca* had struggled back across the Atlantic to England.

According to an official statement made by the ship's uni-auricular captain, the sundered organ was handed back to him immediately after its amputation. In March 1738, Jenkins is reputed to have been hawking the offending article around Parliament, in pickled form. If the tale is to be believed, he had been ordered to appear at the House of Commons so that members of parliament could hear with their own ears how Jenkins came to be parted from one of his. When questioned as to his reaction at the time of the outrage, the captain is said to have avowed, with a sententiousness he must have felt the occasion demanded, 'I commended my soul to God and my cause to my country.'

A full eight years after the event, this humiliation suffered by one of George II's subjects was – somewhat conveniently – deemed tantamount to an attack on Britain herself and ample cause to embark on yet another war with Spain.

Of course, there were many other reasons why British politicians and their king were keen for hostilities to break out again. For one thing, there was the matter of rival imperial conquests in North

America. It was also in British interest to increase trade with the colonies on the continent and it was a cause of frustration that the Spanish restricted such activities. Nevertheless, however unlikely it may seem, the ear became a lightning rod for British anger at supposed Spanish aggression and wrongdoings. Prime Minister Sir Robert Walpole found himself hemmed in on all sides by those clamouring for the restoration of British pride, which was something the hawks claimed could only be achieved through military conflict. Somewhat reluctantly he bowed to the pressure and, in 1739, Britain and Spain were once again at war.

The fighting was concentrated in the Caribbean – principally attacks on ports in North America, Venezuela, Panama and New Granada (now part of Colombia) – with the two sides squaring up to one another rather inconclusively. Three years later, back in Europe, the War of the Austrian Succession broke out. This was a messy dispute that began with Prussia and Austria quarrelling over ownership of Silesia but widened as other European powers had inevitably piled in on either side. There was a good possibility that France might cement her own position as the pre-eminent power in Europe and there were even well-grounded fears in Britain that a Franco-Spanish invasion was imminent. The British, who were not keen that any of this should come to pass, had taken the side of Austria. Thus, the War of Jenkins' Ear became subsumed into this broader conflict that was being fought much closer to home. The Treaty of Aix-la-Chapelle (one of whose negotiators was the Earl of Sandwich, see page 74) brought the latter to a conclusion in 1748. By extension, this ended the War of Jenkins' Ear as well, though operations in the Americas had largely fizzled out a few years beforehand anyway.

Another curious thing about this particular conflict is that its name was only coined a century or so after the event. The essayist Thomas Carlyle first used the term in 1858 in his *History of Friedrich II of Prussia*. Perhaps he had an eye on fixing this particular dispute – which had simply been known as one of the Anglo-Spanish wars – firmly in the mind of his readers. He had good reason to do so because there is a dazzling array of Anglo-Spanish wars given the name 'The Anglo-Spanish War' and differentiated merely by the dates of their occurrence. It is apt to confuse at the best of times and so at least Carlyle managed to pull one from the mire and make it memorable.

Despite the fact that the War of Jenkins' Ear proved to be little more than a disjointed series of indecisive military actions and an excuse for 'privateers' (that is, state-sponsored pirates) on both sides to prey on each other's shipping, the conflict did have long-lasting repercussions. It set a precedent in that it involved a regiment formed of American colonists being incorporated into the British Army and then packed off to fight somewhere other than North America. This would become yet one more grievance to add to the pile of American resentments regarding British rule.

Secondly, it drove Spain and France into an alliance that would last nearly a century and contribute to Britain's loss of its North American colonies in 1783.

Finally, as the historian Harold Temperley argued, the war had been the first that Britain had conducted in which 'the trade interest absolutely predominated, in which the war was waged solely for balance of trade rather than for balance of power'. Over 250 years later, the accusation is repeatedly made that Prime Minister Tony Blair led Britain into the second Iraq War for economic not moral reasons. Certainly, it's difficult to believe that quite so much enthusiasm for 'regime change' would have been generated had Iraq been a major producer of kale rather than oil. Perhaps, in a hundred years' time, some historian will call the invasion of Iraq 'The War of the Sexed-Up Dossier' and it will stick.

As for the two players in the drama that helped bring about the War of Jenkins' Ear, Juan de León Fandiño was captured with his ship in 1742 and sent under guard to Portsmouth. Meanwhile Robert Jenkins went back to sea as captain of a ship in the East India Company, an organisation that was about to make its own devastating mark on history (see page 22).

Robert Clive reaches for an unreliable pistol

It's an irony that the world's largest-ever empire owes so much to a weapon that failed to work rather than the countless ones used on its behalf that did. A recurring fault in a pistol owned by an obscure teenager not only helped kick-start the British Empire, it had a greater effect on the last 300 years of Indian history than any single event other than the birth of Mahatma Gandhi.

Robert Clive, a tearaway lad packed off to India by his father, was only 18 or 19 when he attempted to commit suicide. Bored, homesick and often falling foul of his employers, he was gripped with a terrible depression. One day, unable to abide it any longer, he took out his pistol, aimed it at his head and pulled the trigger. Nothing happened. He steeled himself afresh, pressed the gun to his head and pulled the trigger again. Once more, the gun refused to fire. Seized with the notion that these two occurrences were a sign that the Fates had spared him – and that they would not have done so without reason – the young man put the gun away and resolved to achieve some great work with his life.

It is now believed by many historians that Clive suffered from bipolar disorder and that this attempt at suicide occurred at a time when his mental illness had thrown him into a deep depression. Certainly he had exhibited very chaotic behaviour up to that point and, as events 30 years later were to show, he remained susceptible to bouts of depression.

The future 1st Baron Clive of Plassey was born to Rebecca and Richard Clive at Styche Hall, near Market Drayton, Shropshire, on 29 September 1725. The family lived on a small estate that had been passed down the generations since it had been granted to them by Henry VII. Several members of the family had gone on to secure a name for themselves in public office, with Robert's father serving as MP for Montgomeryshire. Robert himself was one of 13 children, only seven of whom survived past infancy, and at no point in his childhood did he show any signs whatsoever that he might replicate the minor glories of his forebears.

His parents, unable to afford the upkeep of Styche Hall and feed their many children, sent Robert away to Manchester at the age of three to be fostered by childless relatives. There he was so spoiled that when he returned to his parents six years later he was completely ungovernable. Indeed, it's a wonder that he didn't end up in prison. He progressed from bizarre anti-social behaviour such as climbing the tower of a local church to sit on a gargoyle and leer at anyone who passed by, to setting up and running a protection racket, terrorising the shopkeepers of Market Drayton into handing over money to his gang of teenage hoodlums. Along the way, he contrived to get himself expelled from three schools.

It's not entirely surprising, therefore, that his father despaired of the young Robert. He secured his wayward son a job as a clerk with the East India Company and sent him off to India in March 1743. Robert had only been at this posting for a year or so when his attempted suicide took place.

Spurred by the belief that his life had been spared for a purpose, Robert wasted no time in putting himself in a situation where he might end the lives of others. He signed up for military service with the East India Company's private army, received his commission as an ensign, and before long took part in various battles against the French, Britain's arch-rival in the struggle for colonial supremacy in India. He soon gained a reputation for valour and by 1749 he was made captain of commissary. This put him in charge of the supply of provisions to British forces in India and he was not blind to the possibilities the position afforded him, quickly amassing a personal fortune. Clearly you can take the boy out of Market Drayton but you can't take Market Drayton out of the boy.

Two years later, he volunteered his services to help relieve Trichinopoly where Mohammed Ali, Britain's preferred choice for *nawab* (local ruler), was being besieged by the French choice, Chanda Sahib. With just 500 men, Clive captured the latter's capital, Arcot, forcing Chanda Sahib to send 10,000 of his troops back from Trichinopoly to attempt to retake it. Clive held out for 50 days in Arcot until reinforcements arrived, then started a guerrilla campaign against the French forces and their allies. Trichinopoly was eventually relieved and Mohammed Ali was confirmed as *nawab*, his status eventually being recognised twelve years later in the Treaty of Paris of 1763. This effectively gave Britain (in the guise of the East India Company) control of southern India.

In 1753, Clive sailed back to Britain in triumph, fêted as a military hero whom future Prime Minister William Pitt the Elder would hail as a 'heaven-born general'. His reputation and riches (an estimated £234,000) made him quite the eligible young man – he was still only 27 on his return. He married a woman named Margaret Maskelyne and began to restore Styche Hall to its former glories. Running out of money by 1755, he went back to India, now elevated to the rank of lieutenant-colonel and deputy governor of Fort St David. His actions over the following five years were to leave their mark on both India and Britain for the next two centuries.

His first move was to seize back Calcutta, which had been captured by the *nawab* of Bengal, Siraj ud Daula. The *nawab*'s soldiers had been responsible for the notorious Black Hole of Calcutta incident, in which 123 British troops died of heat stroke or suffocation in a vastly overcrowded cell. However, Clive's greatest victory was yet to come.

In 1757, he persuaded Siraj ud Daula's military commander, Mir Jafar, to switch allegiances – promising to make him *nawab* if he did so. On 23 June, after a couple of days of hesitation, Clive's 3,000 troops – two-thirds of whom were sepoys – attacked Siraj ud Daula's roughly 70,000-strong army, a force that was backed by French artillery. Mir Jafar duly betrayed his master, leading away a very large proportion of the *nawab*'s soldiers, and Clive's humble outfit won the day, suffering fewer than 100 casualties. Mir Jafar was rewarded with the nawabship of Bengal. The Mughal emperor of India, Shah Alam, was forced to sign a document that handed over the task of collecting taxes in Bengal to the East India Company. Mir Jafar rewarded – or was coerced into rewarding – his English co-conspirator, filling Clive's coffers to bursting point (when he returned to Britain in 1760 his fortune had grown to around £2.5m – worth £23m today). Britain, or the East India Company – the distinction was often blurred – had become the supreme power in India and had begun the process of sucking it dry of its wealth and resources, starting by emptying the contents of the treasury of Bengal into 100 boats and sailing off with it.

Clive went on to further successes, both in India and Britain, becoming governor of Bengal (twice), an Irish peer, a knight, a member of parliament for Shrewsbury and later its mayor, and the 1st Baron Clive of Plassey. He bade farewell to India for the final time in 1767.

His vast wealth and the morally ambiguous means – to say the least – by which he had acquired it led to him becoming embroiled in a protracted trial in Britain on corruption charges. He was eventually acquitted, but questions concerning his integrity were raised right up until the end of his life.

It may have been a combination of his physical and mental health problems that led to Clive's death in 1774 at the age of 49. He suffered with stomach pains – for which he took opium in ever-larger doses – and appears to have been afflicted by the depression that had been his unwelcome companion for much of his adult life.

On 22 November 1774, his body was discovered at his Berkeley Square home in London. It is more than likely that he took his own life (though his family strongly denied it at the time). If that was the case, the suicide was hushed up, in part to avoid a scandal but also to allow a burial in consecrated ground. Robert Clive lies today in the churchyard of St Margaret's at Moreton Say, Shropshire, his last resting place unmarked but for a plaque nearby that bears the legend *Primus in Indis* ('First in India').

We therefore cannot be absolutely certain about how Clive came to die – it is variously rumoured that he took an overdose; slit his throat with a paperknife; or shot himself, the Fates failing to intervene a second time. Had Clive's first attempt been as successful, the course of British, Indian and French history would almost certainly have taken a very different turn. India might have avoided the wholesale pillaging of her wealth, the devastating famines caused by Clive's agricultural policies, and the legacy he left: two centuries of the Raj. France might well have seen her own influence in India flourish rather than being unceremoniously snuffed out. And as for Clive's influence on Britain, the former troubled tearaway is credited not only with securing India as a vassal state for the nation but also with providing the impetus for the creation of the British Empire. This in turn gave Britain the wherewithal to finance the Industrial Revolution and maintain its place as a major power into the 20th century.

According to historian William Dalrymple, Clive's activities in India would also inadvertently furnish the English language with a new word. A Hindustani slang term was popularised in Britain in the late 18th century and lives on today: 'loot'.

The freighter *Vigilancia* sinks off the coast of Cornwall

It is a truth universally acknowledged that the attack by Japan on Pearl Harbor triggered the United States' entry into the Second World War. It is a truth almost as universally acknowledged that the event that caused the US to make its equally belated appearance in the First World War was the sinking of the RMS *Lusitania*. The Cunard liner was torpedoed by a German submarine off the south coast of Ireland, causing the death of nearly 1,200 passengers and crew. If evidence of the influence of this atrocity were required, one need only point to the famous American recruitment poster of the time, which bore the legend 'REMEMBER THE LUSITANIA,' and ended with the stern injunction: 'It is your duty to take up the sword of justice to avenge this devil's work. ENLIST TO-DAY.'

However, while America declared war against Japan the day after the pummelling of Pearl Harbor, a cursory glance at the date on which the *Lusitania* was sunk – 7 May 1915 – and the date the US declared war on Germany – 6 April 1917 – gives pause for thought. The sinking of the *Lusitania* certainly caused uproar and revulsion in the United States, particularly when it emerged that 128 Americans had lost their lives, but it clearly did not propel the nation into the Great War.

Rather it was a much smaller and now all-but-forgotten tragedy 150 miles off the coast of Cornwall that pushed the US into siding with Britain and her Allies. On the morning of 16 March 1917, a US-registered freighter called the *Vigilancia*, carrying goods from New York to Le Havre, was torpedoed and sunk by a German submarine. Fifteen mariners lost their lives. Unlike the outrage perpetrated in 1915 on the *Lusitania* (and several other American vessels) by Germany, the sinking of the *Vigilancia* was deemed an act of war and President Woodrow Wilson acted accordingly.

Oberleutnant Otto Wünsche, commander of the German submarine *U-70*, was patrolling the Atlantic that Friday morning in search of enemy shipping. Roughly six weeks beforehand, the orders he received regarding the rules of engagement had changed. In the aftermath of the sinking of the *Lusitania* and another liner called the *Arabic*, the imperial German government had come to an accommodation with the United States that restricted the activities of German submarines with regard to American shipping. However, from 1 February 1917, Germany announced a radical change from that policy. It ordered its submarines to attack and destroy, without warning, every vessel in the 'war zone' that it had declared around both Britain and France, and in the Mediterranean.

In response, President Wilson broke off relations with Germany two days later but stated that he would take no stronger measures unless American shipping was attacked. That same day, the submarine *U-53* sank the American-owned merchant ship *Housatonic* (by a grim twist of fate, the same name as the first ever ship to have been sunk by a submarine – in 1864 during the American Civil War). The U-boat commander involved, Leutnant Hans Rose, was famous for his chivalry, and had not only allowed the crew to disembark before he torpedoed their ship but had towed their lifeboats towards land and drawn the attention of a British naval patrol boat to their plight before heading off. No lives were lost. Given these circumstances, it was difficult to categorise the attack as an act of war, particularly as the *Housatonic* was carrying grain to Germany's enemy, Britain.

Two other American-owned vessels, the *Lyman M. Law* and the *Algonquin*, were subsequently attacked by German submarines, but again their crews had been allowed to board lifeboats before their ships were sunk and there was no loss of life. An intercepted telegram from the German foreign minister to the German ambassador in the US – the so-called Zimmermann Note – was not interpreted as an act of war either, even though it revealed German plans to help Mexico regain Texas, Arizona and New Mexico from the United States (all of which had been lost in the Mexican American War of 1846–48).

It took the actions of Oberleutnant Wünsche to push the United States over the edge and into war. It was cold that morning in the Atlantic and the *Vigilancia* was making heavy weather of it in rough seas when she came to the attention of U-boat *U-70*. The first that Captain Frank A. Middleton and the crew of the 4,000-tonne merchantman knew of the submarine's presence was when a lookout reported an unmistakable straight slash cutting through the water – the trace of a torpedo. It missed the ship, passing aft of her. However, 60 seconds later a second torpedo struck the *Vigilancia* amidships, holing her below the waterline.

Four lifeboats were lowered, into which the entire crew of 45 threw themselves. Unfortunately, two boats capsized almost immediately. The members of the other two saved most of those from the nearer of the stricken lifeboats – including the captain. From the further boat, only Assistant Engineer Walter Scott managed the exhausting mile-long swim through heaving seas to safety. In all, 15 men drowned. Nine came from Spain, South America and Greece, while the remaining six were Americans, the first ever to die since the US-German accord following the sinkings of the *Lusitania* and *Arabic*.

The 30 survivors rowed and sailed 150 miles east over the next two days. For some of the first night they were followed by a submarine. This was probably *U-70* lying in wait to attack whatever ship came to the rescue. As it was, both lifeboats eventually made it to Cornwall unaided on Sunday, 18 March. All on board were alive but, understandably, were suffering badly from the effects of their ordeal. The news of the sinking reached the United States the following day.

Two other American-registered ships, the freighter *City of Memphis* and the tanker *Illinois*, were sunk on 17 and 18 March, respectively. However, in their cases there was no loss of life, so although these sinkings added to an emerging picture of German aggression against America in the Atlantic, neither would have proved a *casus belli* – an act justifying a declaration of war.

The *Vigilancia*, with its six American casualties, was a different matter altogether. Wilson hastily called a cabinet meeting for 20 March, and although the deaths of those on the merchant ship were not mentioned specifically, it was telling that those members who had been straining to keep the US out of the war now conceded with heavy hearts that such a course was not only inevitable but necessary for the nation's self-defence. The following day the president convened Congress for 2 April, the earliest practicable date.

Prior to the vote, news of three further losses of American ships had reached Congress. One was to a mine, another was thought to have been caused by a mine (only much later was it correctly attributed to a U-boat), and the third, a freighter called the *Missourian*, had not resulted in any deaths.

In his address to Congress, Wilson couched his appeal for a declaration of war on Germany in broad idealistic terms, citing the defence of moral principles and the right of neutral nations to resist autocratic states. However, early on in his speech he also alluded to the events that had led him to the conclusion that a declaration of war was justified. These included the lives lost on the *Vigilancia* – at the time, the only known American casualties:

> American ships have been sunk, American lives taken, in ways which it has stirred us very deeply to learn of, but the ships and people of other neutral and friendly nations have been sunk and overwhelmed in the waters in the same way. There has been no discrimination. The challenge is to all mankind. Each nation must decide for itself how we will meet it.

There followed four days of debates before a vote was taken on 6 June 1917. The resolution to declare war was carried, though eight senators and fifty congressmen voted against it.

America's entry into the Great War tipped the scales in favour of the Allies. The latter emerged victorious – if such a word can properly be used in relation to so ghastly and needless a conflict – the following year. However, President Wilson had brought his nation into the conflagration only with the greatest reluctance, fearing that the war would change the face of his nation regardless of the outcome. On the eve of the declaration, he told Frank I. Cobb, editor of the *New York World* and close confidant, 'Once lead this people into war and they'll forget there ever was such a thing as tolerance. To fight you must be brutal and ruthless, and the spirit of ruthless brutality will enter into the very fiber of our national life.'

He had a point. Although far from being a peace-loving nation in the 141 years of its existence up to 1917, the United States has taken military action against more than fifty countries since heading into World War I. Furthermore, from 1950 onwards, barely a year has gone by in which the superpower hasn't been bombing someone somewhere. Perhaps the new-found American enthusiasm for building walls instead is actually a step forward.

Leopold Lojka makes a wrong turn

It was the West Midlands philosopher Kevin Rowland who, in his seminal 1980 work 'There, There, My Dear', opined, 'The only way to change things is to shoot men who arrange things.' Never was this viewpoint more convincingly borne out than when Gavrilo Princip gunned down Archduke Franz Ferdinand on a Sarajevo street in June 1914, single-handedly triggering World War I.

And yet it might all have been so different. Had it not been for a lack of communication between a chauffeur and an official regarding the route the archduke's car should take, the assassination would almost certainly not have happened and the planet might thus have been spared not only World War I but World War II as well. Despite the fact that it occurred 1,000 miles away, no other slip-up in communications has had such a drastic effect on the history of the British Isles.

It must be admitted that Europe was something of a tinderbox at the time. A network of alliances had been struck to bolster the continent's competing powers, and tensions were running high on a number of fronts. In the two Balkan Wars of 1912–13, Serbia had wrested control of Kosovo and Macedonia from the Ottoman Empire. A few years beforehand, the little Balkan state of Bosnia had been annexed by the mighty (but creaking) Austro-Hungarian empire. This latter move had been particularly badly received by Bosnia's Serb population, who were adamant that their country should become part of the Serbian kingdom instead.

In the spring of 1914, a small group of young Bosnian Serbs based in Sarajevo discussed how they might bring about this drastic change in the political landscape. One of the members of the band was Gavrilo Princip, a small and rather puny 19-year-old from an obscure and isolated hamlet called Obljaj in the northwest of the country. His father, a peasant farmer who adhered to a strict Christian moral code, had fought against the Ottoman Empire as a young man. Gavrilo started school at the grand old age of nine and was found to be very adept at his studies. He moved to Sarajevo four years later to complete his education.

There he secretly joined *Mlada Bosna* (Young Bosnia), a student organisation dedicated to integrating Bosnia into a Greater Serbia. He became a fan of Bogdan Žerajić, a 24-year-old Bosnian Serb who had committed suicide after making a failed attempt on the life of an Austro-Hungarian governor of Bosnia and Herzegovina. The adolescent would even spend whole nights at Žerajić's grave and it is there that, in his own words, 'I made up my mind sooner or later to perpetrate an outrage.' Expelled from school in 1912 for having taken part in an anti-Austro-Hungarian demonstration, Princip walked roughly 170 miles to the Serbian capital Belgrade with the aim of enlisting to fight against the Ottoman Empire, as his father had done before him.

Rejected because of his diminutive build, he eventually managed to get himself initiated into the arts of war by joining the Serbian Chetnik Organisation, who sent him to a training camp. Returning to Sarajevo, he experienced the 1913 Austro-Hungarian imposition of martial law – an attempt to clamp down on those with pro-Serbian sympathies.

Bridling at this further indignation, Princip and his friends decamped to Belgrade and debated the most effective ways in which they could fight back. A golden opportunity would not be long in coming. The following year it was announced that Archduke Ferdinand – the heir to the Austro-Hungarian throne – would visit Sarajevo to oversee military manœuvres and open a museum. The order had come from Emperor Franz Joseph, the archduke's uncle. Ferdinand knew it was a risky endeavour, since assassination attempts by Serbs on high-ranking officials of the

Austro-Hungarian Empire were not uncommon, and Sarajevo was likely to be home to plenty of citizens who wished to see the emperor's heir dead. His wife Sophie, Duchess of Hohenberg, was only too aware of the danger and insisted on accompanying her husband.

Danilo Ilić, a member of the suitably Machiavellian-sounding secret society Black Hand, recruited two Serbians and one young man from Herzegovina for the assassination. When Princip and two of his friends contacted Serbian military intelligence, they were added to the team. Pistols, bombs, maps, cyanide and further training were supplied by the military intelligence top brass: Dragutin Dimitrijević (commonly known as Apis) and Vojislav Tankosić. These two were cold-blooded killers who had carried out the 1903 assassinations of the Serbian King Alexander I Obrenović and his wife, Queen Draga, in order to place the more nationalistic Peter I on the throne. It was Apis who later admitted to having made the decision to assassinate Franz Ferdinand. Princip, his two friends and their weapons entered Bosnia on 1 June.

On the morning of the fatal day – 28 June 1914 – Ilić places his assassins along the route that the archduke's motorcade would take. They are Muhamed Mehmedbašić and Vaso Čubrilović, who are both in their late twenties; and Cvjetko Popović, Trifko Grabež, Nedeljko Čabrinović and Gavrilo Princip, all of whom are either 18 or 19.

Celebrating their fourteenth wedding anniversary, Archduke Ferdinand and Duchess Sophie arrive at Sarajevo railway station. They are met by a line-up of six cars. The couple is to ride in the third, an open-top Gräf & Stift 28/32 PS Double Phaeto. Aside from a specially-assigned security officer, who takes the leading car, security is left to the local police, who are rather thinly resourced. A suggestion that troops should line the route has been turned down on the grounds that their presence might offend those citizens of Sarajevo who are loyal to the Austro-Hungarian regime.

Following a cursory inspection of a military barracks, the archduke and his retinue head for a reception at the town hall by way of the Appel Quay along the north bank of the River Miljacka. The cars pass Mehmedbašić and Čubrilović but neither react. However, when the motorcade reaches Nedeljko Čabrinović, he throws his bomb. It bounces off the back of the Archduke's car. The bomb's 10-second delay means that it doesn't explode until after the following car is passing over it. Its occupants are badly injured, as are a dozen or more members of the public. Čabrinović downs his cyanide and, just to ensure that he kills himself, jumps into the river. However, his belt-and-braces approach comes to nought. The cyanide has gone beyond its expiry date and has no effect, and the River Miljacka is only a few inches deep, so fails to drown him. He is immediately arrested, receiving a thorough kicking from the crowd for good measure. After a delay to give aid to the wounded, the five undamaged cars continue on their way to the town hall, unmolested by the final three would-be assassins waiting along Appel Quay.

At the town hall, Franz Ferdinand is understandably vexed and chastises the Sarajevo mayor, Fehim Curčić, for the less-than-congenial welcome he has just received. In the meantime, the five undetected conspirators disperse. Princip takes himself off a short way to Moritz Schiller's delicatessen, near a bridge over the Miljacka. This is on the route the motorcade should take later that morning if there is no change in plan. It is difficult to believe, however, that Princip harbours much hope that the archduke's party will stick to its itinerary.

Here we must pull away from the drama for a moment to deal with a 21st-century urban myth that surrounds the climax of the day's events. It is widely believed that Princip had gone into Moritz Schiller's delicatessen to purchase a sandwich. 'If only Princip had not felt peckish that day, and thus had not decided to go and buy a sandwich,' the commonly accepted story goes, 'he would not have been in the right place to shoot the archduke and World War I would have been averted.' It's a compelling story but, unfortunately, there is no contemporary evidence whatsoever that supports it, and plenty that makes it highly unlikely. Furthermore, no one ate sandwiches in Sarajevo in 1914.

By dint of some detective work, historian Mike Dash appears to have discovered the origin of this popular misconception. A novel written by Brazilian television host Jô Soares and titled *Twelve Fingers* (in its English translation of 2001) stars a protagonist called Dimitri who magically appears at major flashpoints of the 20th century. When he turns up in Sarajevo on 28 June 1914, he notices Gavrilo Princip emerging from a market, sandwich in hand. Dimitri engages briefly him in conversation, during which Princip bats away an enquiry about his presence there by claiming he's simply eating a sandwich. The two men part and a little while later Princip carries out the assassination.

The 'sandwich' element to the story was inadvertently popularised by a documentary called *Days That Shook the World*, which was broadcast by the BBC in 2003. It has since become one of the great 'strange but true' events of our times, despite being 'strange but false'.

Anyway, back at the town hall, the mayor and Archduke having both given speeches, there is a debate as to what the party should do next. The archduke's chamberlain favours holing up there and waiting for troops to arrive to protect them. However, the governor of Bosnia and Herzegovina, General Oskar Potiorek, who had been in the archduke's car during the attack, pooh-poohs the idea, allegedly snapping, 'Do you think that Sarajevo is full of assassins?' Ferdinand expresses a desire to go to the hospital, where the injured members of his entourage have been taken and the motorcade duly sets off on its final calamitous journey.

It is at this point that the fateful miscommunication occurs. Potiorek has decided that the cars should head back along Appel Quay to get to the hospital. Unfortunately, in the turmoil, he does not pass this information to Leopold Lojka, who is at the wheel of the Archduke's car, or any of the other drivers. As a result, Lojka turns off Appel Quay onto Franz Joseph Street. He is following the driver in front of him, who is himself following the route to the museum that the Archduke had been intending to open before the plans were thrown into chaos by Čabrinović's bomb.

The disaster might have been averted even then, if Lojka had carried on driving. Instead, Potiorek shouts at him that he has taken a wrong turn and the chauffeur duly pulls to a halt. By chance, the car has stopped directly in front of Moritz Schiller's delicatessen. Hardly able to believe his luck, Gavrilo Princip draws his Browning pistol. He steps out into the road and begins loosing off into the open-topped car. The first bullet slices the archduke's jugular vein. Sophie throws herself in front of her husband to protect him. The second shot, though intended for Potiorek, hits the duchess in the stomach. (Some versions of the event have the first shot hitting Sophie and the second hitting her husband but the result is the same.) Lojka drives off, desperately making for Potiorek's residence so that the couple can receive medical attention. However, they fade together. Sophie succumbs en route, with Franz dying shortly afterwards.

Like Čabrinović, Princip takes his cyanide and meets with the same result. His attempt to shoot himself is foiled by a man named Smail Spahovic. He is beaten up by bystanders, arrested by the police and hauled off to custody.

The chain of events that took place as a result of Leopold Lojka's seemingly innocuous right turn – and the sheer speed of those events – is staggering. Naturally, Serbia and the Austro-Hungarian Empire fell out, all but instantly. The former refused to open an investigation into the killings. Austria-Hungary, with backing from its German ally, sought to exploit the situation by delivering a list of demands to Serbia on 23 July. This became known as the July Ultimatum. The Serbian authorities were given 48 hours to arrest those involved in the plot and take other specified steps to ensure the nation remained on a friendly footing with the empire.

Serbia, backed by Russia, gave a somewhat ambiguous response, agreeing to a couple of points but giving obfuscatory responses to many of the others. The Austro-Hungarian Empire duly cut off diplomatic relations. The following day, Serbian troops crossed the Danube into Austro-Hungarian territory, but were repulsed by soldiers firing above their heads. The next day, on 28 July, the empire declared war on Serbia. This immediately drew Russia and France into the conflict. They were signatories with Serbia to a secret Triple Alliance treaty of 1892, in which all the parties agreed to back each other militarily if attacked. This in turn triggered the mobilisation of the German army in support of Austria-Hungary. The first shots of what would become known as The Great War were fired barely a month after the shots from Gavrilo Princip's Browning. The German attack on neutral Belgium on the night of 3–4 August gave Britain a reason for getting involved. In the Treaty of London, signed in 1839, Britain had pledged to defend Belgium if she were attacked.

It's arguable that no single act committed on British soil has had the same dramatic effect on the nation as the shooting of Archduke Ferdinand in faraway Sarajevo. Certainly, no single slaying, before or since, has had such a disastrous outcome in terms of loss of life. The 'war to end all wars' killed an estimated 15–18 million people, of which around a million were from the United Kingdom (which included the whole of Ireland at the time). The Treaty of Versailles – signed after the war's conclusion – impoverished and emasculated Germany, a state of affairs that was instrumental in paving the way for Adolf Hitler to come to power. He rapidly plunged the planet into a second conflagration, bringing about another 50–70 million violent deaths and speeding up the development and first use of the atom bomb.

Gavrilo Princip was not executed, as might be expected, because at 19 he was too young to receive the death penalty (he fell short by a mere 27 days). Instead he was sentenced to 20 years' imprisonment in the Terezín fortress (also known as Theresienstadt) in Bohemia. The other teenagers in the plot received between 13 and 20 years. Five older members were sentenced to death by hanging.

Princip was not destined to serve a great deal of his term. Kept permanently in chains and in solitary confinement, in the insanitary and spartan conditions prevalent in the fortress his health deteriorated (as did that of Čabrinović and Grabež, who both died of tuberculosis in the early months of 1916). In a famous photograph taken of him at the prison, a sunken-eyed and diminished Princip is almost unrecognisable as the bold, handsome figure pictured outside the courthouse during the trial of the conspirators. He either came down with skeletal tuberculosis in prison or had already contracted it before he arrived. Whichever it was, the conditions of his confinement allowed the wasting disease to flourish, and doctors were forced to amputate his left arm. Princip died on 28 April 1918 at the age of 23, with the war he had brought about still raging beyond his prison walls.

A British soldier shows mercy to a future German Chancellor

It has become something of a cliché that anyone with the power to travel back in time has some sort of bounden duty to attempt to kill Adolf Hitler before 3 September 1939 and thus avert World War II. Leaving aside the difficulties of changing the course of history once it has already occurred, it's curious that such a fatwa is rarely declared on Joseph Stalin (killer of at least 20 million and possibly as many as 60 million of his fellow humans), Mao Tse Tung (at least 45 million) or Jim Davidson.

What is perhaps even more remarkable is that it seems almost certain that one man did indeed have the opportunity to kill Hitler before World War II began and yet did not take it. Of course, since the occasion arose during World War I and the German infantryman lined up in the man's rifle sights was to him just another anonymous *Gefreiter* (the German equivalent of a lance corporal), it is difficult to be too harsh on him. The action took place on 28 September 1918, as the Germans were retreating, having lost the battle for the French village of Marcoing. The 29-year-old Hitler unwittingly stumbled into the British soldier's line of fire. On the point of pulling the trigger, the serviceman realised that the enemy NCO in front of him was wounded and was not making any attempt to fire upon him. Unwilling to kill the man in cold blood, the British soldier lowered his weapon. The future author of *Mein Kampf* nodded his head at him in recognition of his act of clemency and slipped away.

We only know about this story at all because Hitler himself related it to Neville Chamberlain when the two men met in Germany in 1938 during the prime minister's fruitless trip in search of peace. The year before, the Führer had come across a well-known painting by the Italian artist Fortunino Matania showing Private Henry Tandey – famed as the most decorated British soldier of the Great War – carrying a wounded man over his shoulder at the Menin Crossroads in 1914. As soon as he saw it, Hitler believed he recognised Tandey as the man who had spared his life nearly two decades beforehand. He even went as far as requesting a large photograph of the painting from Colonel Earle of the Green Howards, the regiment with which Tandey served. We know that his wish was granted because Captain Weidmann, Hitler's adjutant, wrote a letter of thanks to Earle:

> I beg to acknowledge your friendly gift which has been sent to Berlin through the good offices of Dr Schwend. The Führer is naturally very interested in things connected with his own war experiences, and he was obviously moved when I showed him the picture and explained the thought which you had in causing it to be sent to him. He has directed me to send you his best thanks for your friendly gift which is so rich in memories.

Chamberlain is said to have noticed the photograph of the painting during his visit. Rather taken aback that the German chancellor should be displaying it, he asked him about it. Hitler apparently confided to him: 'That man [Tandey] came so near to killing me that I thought I should never see Germany again. Providence saved me from such devilishly accurate fire as those English boys were aiming at us.'

The German chancellor asked his counterpart to get in touch with Tandey and thank him on his behalf. On returning to Britain, replete with his scrap of paper promising 'peace in our time', the story goes that the prime minister rang Tandey's home to pass on Hitler's gratitude. If this did happen (and it's rather questionable that it did – evidence suggests that Tandey is more likely to have had the news passed on to him at a reunion of the Green Howards)

– it must have come as something of a shock. Reflecting on the episode at Marcoing, Tandey recounted, 'I took aim but couldn't shoot a wounded man so I let him go.' This was typical of the man – he performed this gallant act several times during the war.

It's an astonishing story – how the most decorated British soldier of World War I came within a split second of ending the life of the man who would be instrumental in bringing about its even deadlier sequel. A further bizarre twist is that in one corner of the Matania painting, there are three wounded German prisoners, one of whom does rather resemble Adolf Hitler.

When World War II broke out the year after Chamberlain's visit to Germany, Tandey was filled with regret that he had not killed Hitler when he had had the chance. The incident also rather unfairly tainted his reputation in Britain – he became 'the man who could have shot Hitler'. At the grand old age of 49 he attempted to return to his regiment, the Green Howards. However, he failed his medical on account of the injuries he had received during the war in which he had made his name. Having witnessed the bombing of Coventry and London's Blitz at first hand, he told a reporter at the *Sunday Graphic* newspaper, 'When I saw all the people, women and children he had killed and wounded I was sorry to God I let him go.'

There's just one rather big problem with this story. Although Hitler remembered having his life spared at Marcoing and Tandey remembered sparing a German soldier's life at Marcoing, it is highly unlikely that the two men were recalling the same incident. Tandey's biographer, David Johnson, has pointed out that in 1997, Lt Col Mackintosh of the Green Howards contacted the Bavarian State archives with regard to Hitler's war record in September 1917. They responded that he had been on leave from 25–27 September and that rather than arriving in Marcoing the following morning for his date with destiny, he had already been posted, as Johnson remarks, to 'another part of the line... 50 miles away' on 17 September. So, unless some further evidence emerges that suddenly puts Adolf Hitler in Marcoing on 28 September 1918 after all, the chances are that we'll never know just who it was that came within a hair's breadth of shooting the future demagogue but stayed his trigger finger.

This new information came way too late for Henry Tandey, who died in 1977 at the age of 86. He had spent nearly 40 years of his life regretting that he had not shot Hitler when, in fact, the individual he chose not to kill that day in Marcoing was doubtless just an ordinary soldier doing his best to survive the war so that he could go home to his family.

Of course, had our unknown British soldier pulled *his* trigger when facing *Gefreiter* Hitler rather than showing mercy, there's still no way of saying with any certainty that World War II would have been averted. The Treaty of Versailles would have happened anyway and it was that settlement's strictures and demands that so infuriated the German people. It's possible that some other charismatic leader might have taken advantage of the nation's resentment and swept to power with a message similar to Hitler's. It hardly bears thinking about, but in this scenario, the result might conceivably have been even worse: a fascist, anti-Semitic, Aryan-obsessed leader with a more astute military mind than Hitler's might have become German chancellor and started a world war that he had gone on to win.

A farmer shoots a potato-eating pig

In an attempt to meet the insatiable demands of Britain's pork-devouring carnivores, around ten million pigs are slaughtered each year in the UK alone – many of them returning to consciousness after they are stunned only to be knifed and cast into boiling water while still alive. Further millions destined for British plates meet their fate in Denmark, Germany, the Netherlands and other European countries. This might lead one to the conclusion that, as lives go, those of pigs are of little significance to the British (vegans, vegetarians, pescatarians, Jews, Muslims, Jains, Seventh Day Adventists, some Buddhists and Hindus, and sundry others notwithstanding). Given this, it makes it all the more remarkable that it was the fatal shooting of a single pig back in 1859 that all but caused a war between Britain and the United States, and pushed Canada further along the road to independence.

The dispute had its roots in an ambiguously worded agreement signed by Britain and the US in 1846. The Oregon Treaty was supposed to have set a definitive boundary between the United States and what was then known as British North America (today's Canada). There had been particular friction over the path of the frontier at its western end. The treaty made it plain that the 49th parallel should be used to delineate the two territories.

That was all well and good on the mainland, but when it came to divvying up the islands off the west coast, it all became a bit more tenuous. Britain was to have the enormous Vancouver Island in its entirety, since very little of it actually extended south of the 49th parallel. However, the issue of who had sovereignty over a clutch of much smaller islands in the gulf waters between Vancouver and Vancouver Island proved harder to resolve, since legitimate arguments could be made by both sides as to their ownership. The situation was further complicated by the lack of an accurate map of the islands and the passages between them.

To get around this, the architects of the Oregon Treaty had fudged the issue, stating that the border should run through 'the middle of the channel separating the continent from Vancouver's Island'. Unfortunately, there are two channels to which this wording might be said to refer. If the border ran through the Rosario Strait – as the British maintained – then the island group that included San Juan, Orcas and Lopez belonged to Britain. However, if the wording was interpreted as indicating the Haro Strait, then those islands would become US territory. A commission was set up to settle the issue. Britain offered a compromise, in which she took San Juan and offered the remaining islands to the Americans. This was rejected. The commission was suspended.

As a result, an uneasy stand-off took place on San Juan, an island that measures just 55 square miles. By the time of the porcine-related incident, Britain was well represented on the island by a good many settlers as well as the Hudson's Bay Company, which had substantial salmon-curing and sheep-farming interests there. The Americans, by contrast, had no more than thirty of their citizens established on San Juan. Somewhat surprisingly, relations between the two sets of incomers were reported to be highly cordial.

That all came to an abrupt end on 15 June 1859. An Irishman called Charles Griffin, who worked on the island for the Hudson's Bay Company, kept some free-range black pigs. One of these, a hefty individual by all accounts, trotted happily onto the land of an American farmer called Lyman Cutlar and began digging up and eating his potatoes. Cutlar took exception to this. It was not the first occasion on which pigs had pillaged his crops and he had had enough of it. He raised his gun and shot the pig dead.

Naturally enough, Griffin was not at all happy about this turn of events and sought Cutlar out. An altercation ensued, the details of which are less than certain (the gist of Griffin's argument was apparently that Cutlar should have done more to keep the potatoes out of his pig). We do know that Cutlar offered Griffin $10 in compensation. It was at this point that things began to escalate almost out of control and certainly out of proportion to the injury suffered (unless, of course, you were the pig). The Irishman turned down Cutlar's offer, demanding $100 instead. Cutlar refused to pay what he felt was a wildly exaggerated sum, at which point Griffin reported him to the relevant authorities (those being the relevant British authorities). Cutlar suddenly found himself in danger of being arrested. His fellow countrymen rallied round and sent a petition to the commander of the Department of Oregon, Brigadier-General William S. Harney, calling upon him to protect them militarily.

Harney was no fan of the British, to say the least, and relished the opportunity to confront them. On 27 July, a company of 66 soldiers of the US 9th Infantry were sent to San Juan with orders to repulse any retaliatory landing by British forces. James Douglas, who was at the time the governor of both the Colony of Vancouver Island and the Colony of British Colombia, was told of the incursion and his response was to dispatch three warships to the island. It was the beginning of a build-up of forces on both sides. The British far outnumbered their opponents though the Americans had the advantage of actually occupying San Juan. By 10 August, the British had five warships bristling with 70 guns and carrying 2,140 troops facing the Americans' 14 cannon and 461 soldiers. Both sides were simply waiting for the other to fire the first shot.

When the commander-in-chief of the British navy in the Pacific, Rear-Admiral Robert L. Baynes, arrived on the scene, Douglas ordered him to send marines onto the island to drive the American troops off it. It was at this late juncture that common sense prevailed, as well as a long-overdue sense of perspective.

Baynes refused point-blank to carry out Douglas' command, declaring that he would not 'involve two great nations in a war over a squabble about a pig'.

It was only at this point that the governments of the two nations became aware of what was going on in their name. President James Buchanan and Prime Minister Lord Stanley, both of whom were keen to prevent military conflict, demanded that negotiations be set in motion. While these were established it was agreed that the British would station around 100 soldiers on the north coast of San Juan while the Americans had the same number in the far south. By all accounts, relations between the members of the opposing camps on the island returned to the genial state that had prevailed before Lyman Cutlar had lost his temper with the pig.

Like the mills of God, the mills of diplomacy grind slowly, and the dispute would not be resolved for another 13 years. The US and Britain signed the Treaty of Washington in 1871, one element of which was an agreement to settle the dispute by appointing international arbitrators. Kaiser Wilhelm I of Germany (grandfather of Wilhelm II of World War I fame) was duly chosen to lead the commission. A year later, the three-man adjudication team he appointed declared that the Haro Strait should be the designated frontier between British North America and the United States, meaning that San Juan fell entirely within US territory. Britain withdrew her troops on 25 November 1872. By that time, both the Colony of Vancouver Island and the Colony of British Colombia had joined the brand-new Dominion of Canada.

While the loss of an obscure island off the coast of one of their many colonies might have been a pill that caused the British a moment's bitterness in swallowing, it was very hard indeed for their dominion's politicians and populace to take. Although the dispute had the virtue of settling once and for all the frontier between the United States and Canada, the fiasco left the

Canadians – already upset by some of the contents of the Oregon Treaty – feeling that their masters in London had not looked after their interests. The Pig War was thus another stepping stone towards Canadian independence from Britain, a journey that would eventually be completed in 1982.

Food

If it's true that we are what we eat, there are few things more important than the choices of food available to us. While many of today's dishes and foodstuffs have developed through a steady process of evolution, some of the mainstays of the British diet have come into being quite by accident. The way food is produced and marketed has even had an impact outside the kitchen, exploding into the world beyond and leaving its spattered mark on entities as diverse as the Industrial Revolution and the nation's legal system.

A physicist demonstrates his invention for softening bones

Back in the 1670s, all Denis Papin wanted to do was find a way of thickening sauces and drawing marrowfat from bones. It did not seem like much to ask and so he set about his task with all the vigour and assurance of a physicist who had a medical degree and who was collaborating in London with the great Robert Boyle, of Boyle's Law fame. The contraption Papin came up with in 1679, he called the 'New Digester or Engine for Softening Bones'. Its novelty was that it cooked its contents under pressure.

Full of excitement, the Frenchman took himself off to the Royal Society to show his prototype to the great men of learning (and naturally it *was* all men – the society's first women would not be elected until 1945). His demonstration was a success. The machine cooked animal bones under pressure until they were reduced to three components: marrowfat, a residue that could be added to sauces to thicken them, and bone made so frangible that it could be ground into meal with ease.

Papin is a classic example of an inventor striving for one thing, only to find that the wider application of their creation completely overshadows their original, much humbler intention. Once he had added a valve that released steam and thus negated the possibility of his machine exploding, Papin had not only effectively invented the pressure cooker, he had also produced the inspiration for a much more important innovation. Just 18 years later, in 1697, the English engineer Thomas Savery would use the piston design from Papin's New Digester as the basis for the world's first steam engine. Savery's creation would in turn be adapted by Thomas

Newcomen in 1712 as a means of pumping water from a mine. Scotsman James Watt would improve on it in his workshop in the grounds of Kinneil House in the 1760s, and in the following decade the Industrial Revolution would be furnished with one of its most potent drivers.

Papin is also a classic example of an inventor who received neither due credit for his invention nor the financial reward his efforts merited. Developing his work on the pressure cooker, he produced plans for an atmospheric steam engine a full 22 years before Newcomen constructed his own version. In 1704 he built the world's first steam-powered vehicle – a paddle steamer – and had the first-ever steam cylinder cast. Seven years later a paper he sent to the Royal Society set out his ideas on what he called Hessian Bellows. This is now recognised as the foundation for the invention of the blast furnace. None of these achievements succeeded in making Papin's name.

To make matters considerably worse, as a Huguenot, he was persecuted in his native France. In 1685, Louis XIV revoked the Edict of Nantes – which had previously granted religious freedom – and Papin went into exile, alternating between England and Germany. He was last heard of in 1712.

The Royal Society retains a letter he wrote to them in January that year. A couple of weeks previously, the organisation had voted to give him £10 for the many services he had rendered them over the years. The letter makes it clear that Papin was still waiting to receive this money. The 64-year-old physicist had no relatives in London to support him and was living in penury. Nothing is known of his fate after he wrote the letter. He was buried on 26 August 1713, in the churchyard at St Bride's in Fleet Street, London.

At least Papin got the last laugh, albeit posthumously: while steam engines have largely been relegated to the realm of heritage railways and industrial museums, his pressure cooker is still used by cooks all over the world.

The Duc de Richelieu's chef cannot find any cream

You do not have to go back far in British social history – the 1970s is far enough – to discover a civilisation in which the very mention of the word 'mayonnaise' was treated with the utmost suspicion. Like all food that came with a French appellation, mayonnaise was imagined to be some sort of mystical substance, the kind of extreme preparation one might only encounter in the pages of a book by Elizabeth David. It was looked on in Britain as a foodstuff – if one could give it that name – that was almost certainly poisonous to everyone who ate it – except the French, whose stomachs had been designed differently. At best, mayonnaise was viewed as an unnecessarily pretentious version of salad cream, which was a dressing that had been made sufficiently bland and uninteresting that it achieved great popularity in Britain.

Today, mayonnaise has become a normal part of everyday British life, a staple at barbecues and an oft-seen companion at picnics. It has moved beyond the delicatessen to carve its own niche on the shelves of corner shops up and down the land. This colonisation of Britain by a whipped-up egg-yolk-oil-vinegar-and-seasoning dressing is due largely to the efforts of her American cousins (at whose vanguard stands Richard Hellmann) and, of course, the daytime radio presenter Simon Mayo.

Despite all this, few Britons stop to think how mayonnaise got its name, or even how this particular confection came to exist at all. Its origins would appear to go back to the aftermath of a siege that took place on the island of Menorca (known as Minorca to the British) during the Seven Years War.

Menorca – which, with Majorca, Ibiza and Formentera, forms the Balearic Isles – lies off the east coast of Spain. An island of some 270 square miles, it has changed hands many times down the ages. In the mid-18th century it happened to belong to the British, who really had no business owning anything at all in the Mediterranean but who had got lucky in backing the winning side in the War of the Spanish Succession and had taken possession of it in 1713 under the terms of the Treaty of Utrecht, one of the many European ententes that were to turn countless future schoolchildren off history forever.

The Seven Years War broke out in 1754. It was orchestrated by Britain, which opened hostilities against France, but it ended up dragging in most of the Continent's major players. Two years into the war, the French, not unreasonably, decided to take the opportunity afforded by the conflict to renew their sovereignty over Menorca, an island whose excellent natural harbour at the capital, Mahón, made it a place of strategic importance.

The 60-year-old Duc de Richelieu, Louis François Armand de Vignerot du Plessis, was chosen for the task. He landed 15,000 troops on the island and laid siege to Fort St Philip, which was held by a garrison that was roughly a fifth of the size of the French force. In response, the British authorities called on Admiral John Byng to set sail for the Mediterranean island to lift the siege. He was given pitifully few resources with which to do so – just ten rather leaky ships. Byng protested loud and hard that he was being sent on a mission that had very little chance of succeeding but his objections were ignored. He half-heartedly engaged the French fleet on 19 May 1756. No ships were lost on either side before the French fleet withdrew, but roughly 40 sailors were killed on each side. Byng headed back to Gibraltar, seeking repairs to his ships.

After three months, with no end to the siege in sight, the British force in Fort St Philip surrendered and, rather sportingly, were accorded safe passage off the island. The Duc de Richelieu was naturally in high spirits after the victory, which had been gained at comparatively little loss of life. He ordered a great banquet to celebrate his triumph. Such a feast would naturally entail the rustling up of lashings of an egg-yolk-and-cream dressing of which the duke was particularly enamoured.

Unfortunately – perhaps because the island's cows had been moved a safe distance from the siege – there was no cream to be had. This left the duke's head chef in something of a quandary. It is not known whether he himself hit upon the idea of substituting olive oil for the cream, or whether a Menorcan suggested it to him. The latter is a distinct possibility since the island was well known for its aïoli. This is a similar dressing to mayonnaise, being an emulsion of olive oil and lemon juice to which egg yolk and a great deal of garlic is added – but no cream. Whatever happened, the newfangled sauce was hailed at the banquet as a roaring success. It was only natural that it should be christened with a name that would forever fix the location of that glorious victory in the French language. That location was Mahón and thus Richelieu himself is said to have named the dressing 'sauce mahonnaise', a term whose spelling drifted later to 'mayonnaise'.

It must be admitted that there's a clutch of other stories that proffer alternative origins for the sauce and its name. One is simply that it comes from the Old French word *moyeu* meaning 'yolk'. Another is that mayonnaise was invented in the town of Bayonne in the southwest of France, and that over the years 'sauce Bayonnaise' transmuted into *'sauce Mayonnaise'* (though there seems to be no indication of where or when this crossover took place).

And finally there is the tale of Charles de Lorraine, the Duc de Mayenne. The leader of the Catholic League is said to have been a devotee of the egg-based sauce. Indeed, he was so much of a fan that he allegedly arrived late to the Battle of Arques in 1589 because he had tarried so long over a dish of chicken slathered in 'mayennaise' and the battle was lost as a result. Consequently, his enemy, King Henry IV of France, held on to the key port of Dieppe, but since the duke purportedly ended up with his favourite sauce being named after him, there were no losers.

Unfortunately, as with the other two rival explanations, there is no solid evidence to back any of these stories beyond their linguistic similarities with the word 'mayonnaise'. Furthermore, the battle raged on and off for 15 days, and only ended when 4,000 English troops, sent by Elizabeth I, arrived in support of Henry IV, so a defeat caused by a short delay to eat a delicious sauce seems somewhat far-fetched. As a result, most food historians and dictionary compilers opt for the Mahón tale as the most likely source of mayonnaise.

It was only a pity for the French that, when Britain gained the upper hand in the Seven Years War, the terms of the Treaty of Paris returned Menorca to British hands just seven years after it was lost. Since the Treaty of Amiens in 1802, the island has been Spanish. It has far more chance of joining with a future independent Catalonia to form a new nation than ever becoming French again. Still, if nothing else, the dressing maintains the sweet savour of revenge. The British may crow interminably about their victories over the French, as witnessed in Trafalgar Square and Waterloo Station, but the French have conquered huge parts of the world with their mayonnaise.

An artist creates a lemon juice container that looks exactly like a lemon

'The law,' opined the Scottish writer Dr Arbuthnot, at a time when it was already considered clichéd to think of it as merely an ass, 'is a bottomless pit.'

In one way, it would be good if this were true. While the author of *The History of John Bull* certainly intended his observation to be taken as a condemnation, it could just about be interpreted as an accolade: that its limitless depths allow the law to accommodate every kind of malefactor, from the pettiest of petty criminals to the head of state who perpetuates the most heinous war crimes. Sadly though, this has never been true and it is unlikely that it will ever become so.

But even if the law often fails to bring down the world's most reprehensible villains, one can still admire its sheer scope. No matter how obscure or contrived a circumstance, there is almost always a statute out there somewhere that can be brought to bear on it. Take, for example, the curious case of Reckitt & Colman Ltd vs Borden Inc: a three-year court battle over a plastic lemon juice container that was every bit as bitter as its contents and which ended up setting a legal precedent.

The story begins with a man called William Alec Gibson Pugh. An art-school graduate from East Ham in London, Pugh was in his mid-twenties when he was headhunted in 1947 by a Leicestershire company called Cascelloid. Hoping to put the company at the forefront of the revolution in plastics, Cascelloid had imported a cutting-edge machine from the United States that was able to manufacture bottles by blowing plastic – only one other machine of its kind existed in the world at the time.

Using his artistic talents, Pugh began to experiment with original designs for bottles, his first being a teddy bear that contained baby powder. Later on in his career he was to fashion the famous fist-sized tomatoes that served as ketchup dispensers in cafés up and down the land. His finest hour, however, came in the 1950s when Cascelloid was approached by a company called Edward Hack Ltd. Their executives were keen to develop a novelty bottle to boost sales of their lemon juice.

According to his obituary in the *Independent*, Pugh carved a wooden core onto which he painstakingly stuck fresh lemon peel. Once he had the shape just right, he made a plaster mould of it. The result was a squeezy plastic lemon-juice container that was not only the size and colour of a lemon but looked exactly like a lemon (albeit one with a capped nozzle at one end) – details that were to cause something of a legal tangle decades later. Edward Hack found instant success selling its lemon juice in the plastic lemon at a shilling a time, under the brand name Hax.

Word of the innovation crossed the Atlantic, and soon several copycat plastic lemons filled with lemon juice were on sale in the United States. However, since Hax was not sold in America, there was no question of bringing legal proceedings against these companies for infringing design rights. In the meantime, Reckitt & Colman bought up Edward Hack and Hax was renamed Jif.

All went quietly onwards until the 1980s when a US firm called Borden, which sold its lemon juice in squeezy plastic lemons under the name ReaLemon, decided to start selling its product to Britain. Reckitt & Colman took exception to this and a writ was served. It was at this point that Bill Pugh's attention to detail was suddenly recognised by the plaintiff's lawyers as something of a problem. The Jif lemon looked just like a natural lemon – just as it was supposed to do. It meant that there was nothing about it that made it recognisably a Reckitt & Colman-style lemon, and thus it was impossible to register as a trademark.

The case dragged on, passing up through the courts until it ended up at the House of Lords. A judgment was finally handed down in 1990, with the lords unanimously finding in favour of Reckitt & Colman.

The case is of lasting importance because of a three-part test on trademark infringement set out by Lord Oliver of Aylmerton, which has been handily summarised by Ernie Smith in the newsletter *Tedium*:

1. There must be an existing reputation that the public carries with the original product or design.

2. The competing product creates confusion or misrepresentation in the market, whether intentional or not.

3. There are signs that the confusion created by the competing product negatively impacts the bottom line of the original one.

As Lord Oliver succinctly put it, in his legal opinion: 'Thus A can compete with B by copying his goods, provided that he does not do so in such a way as to suggest that his goods are those of B.'

The *Law Society Gazette* made a note of the case at the time: 'Because it is a natural shape, a lemon cannot be registered as a design. But the Lords accepted that consumers were more likely to buy the lemon on account of shape rather than read the product's label.'

All was not lost for Borden – the only thing it needed to do was change its own design sufficiently so that there was no longer any confusion between its ReaLemon and Reckitt & Colman's Jif (since acquired by corporate leviathan Unilever) and it could carry on selling its product.

This unlikely lemon-juice war provided British jurisprudence with a landmark case that can now be referred to whenever a company is accused of passing off its brand as that of a more successful competitor. Had Bill Pugh not been a perfectionist, it may never have come to pass.

There is evidence to suggest that Pugh's lemon had itself been preceded by a similar plastic container emanating from Italy. Therefore it's quite possible that the law-defining plastic lemon may yet have another day in court, and go on to define another nation's laws.

A Spanish ship containing oranges is battered by a North Sea storm

Crossing the Channel to the Continent, one of the many differences to Blighty that the doughty British traveller will notice – aside from how cheery everyone looks – is in the meaning of the term 'marmalade'. Pick up a jar with that word on the label in a French *épicerie*, for example, and it will not contain an orange, jelly-like substance, flecked with pieces of peel, but something more akin to a fruit paste, and probably one that will not have any connection with an orange at all.

Scurry down to a grocer's in Portugal and there is likely to be more scratching of heads and fruitless repetitions of the word because their *marmelada* – from which the English word 'marmalade' is derived – is specifically a quince paste (*marmelo* being the Portuguese for quince). The story is the same on other parts of the Continent. In order to secure a jar of the orange preserve that sweetens the toast of Britons from Aberdeen to Zennor, the wanderer will have to ask specifically for *marmelade d'oranges* in France and *marmellata di arance amare* ('marmalade of bitter oranges') in Italy.

Back in the late Middle Ages, variations of the term 'marmalade' were used throughout Europe to describe all kinds of fruit pastes. Though quinces were the standard ingredient, many other fruits were turned into a marmalade, mixed with some combination of honey, sugar and spices. At this time, marmalade was a catch-all term that covered everything from chunks of fruit preserved in a syrup to a fully fledged fruit paste, and could include honey, spices, rose water or even musk and ambergris. The English had their own variation, known as 'chardequince', which was rather viscous and employed cinnamon and other spices.

Even later English marmalades would barely be recognisable to modern Britons. A recipe for 'Marmelet of Oranges' is included in a handwritten book found in Cheshire and dating from about 1677. The author, Eliza Cholmondeley, sets out instructions for a preserve that uses only bitter oranges and sugar, and results in a sweet fruit paste.

It's not until the 18th century that one finds something resembling the translucent jelly-like substance that goes by the name marmalade today. Mary Kettilby's comprehensive tome *A Collection of Above Three Hundred Receipts in Cookery, Physick and Surgery*, published around 1714, contains a marmalade recipe that includes lemon juice and instructs cooks to boil the mixture 'until it will jelly'. Even so, such delicacies were too expensive to become popular and so tended to be the preserve of the wealthy.

The classic British marmalade would not have taken over the nation's breakfast tables had it not been for a storm at sea. One day, in the 18th century, a ship carrying Seville oranges from Spain began to make heavy weather of it as the winds whipped up the shallow waters of the North Sea. Although probably bound for Leith, from where its cargo could be carted to markets in Edinburgh, the captain decided to avoid the Firth of Forth and put in at the port of Dundee. Rather than have his Seville oranges rot in their crates as he waited for a favourable turn in the weather, the captain decided to cut his losses and sell them off cheaply where he was. He just happened to have chosen the city where one of the inhabitants was a woman who would change the face of the British breakfast: Janet Keiller.

It's at this point that things begin to get a little cloudy. According to C. Anne Wilson's excellent *The Book of Marmalade*, there are two possible Janet Keillers of Dundee who might have been that woman. One (Janet Pierson) is known to have married a James Keiller in 1700. Another, Janet Matthewson, married John Keiller, who was a descendent of the first couple. To confuse things further, Janet and John had a son called James, thus producing a second James Keiller. Both husbands appear to have run a grocer's shop in the city, possibly one that was passed down through the generations. Unfortunately, the one key fact that could settle the argument – the year in which the ship got caught in the storm – is not known. For what it's worth, the Keiller Company's own history plumps for the later Janet and, as we shall see, she does seem the more likely one.

What we can be more certain of is that the husband of one of the Janets, a man with an eye for a bargain, caught wind of the sale. He availed himself of a good quantity of the oranges, taking some of them home to his wife. Unlike the normal run of oranges, the Seville orange has a bitter taste and is not the sort of fruit that was likely to fly off the shelves of the Keillers' shop. This left husband and wife with something of a problem.

Janet Keiller decided that the best thing to do in these circumstances would be to make the oranges into marmalade, which would at least preserve them. In order to spare herself the wearisome task of pounding the oranges down to a pulp, she cut the peel into chips before boiling it up with sugar and lemon juice. Janet's 'Dundee Orange Marmalade' proved very popular with customers, and soon fresh supplies of Seville oranges were being ordered from Spain.

In due course – in 1797, to be precise – the later Janet's boy set up the firm James Keiller and Son in order to sell the marmalade on a larger scale. The Keillers were the first owners of a marmalade factory, cooking up the sweetmeat in large copper pans and selling it at prices that made it accessible to working people for the very first time. Copycat operations sprang up in Dundee, adopting Janet Keiller's 'chip-cut' gelatinous style of marmalade, and the Scottish city became the marmalade capital of Britain. Sales boomed in the first half of the 19th century.

Although it cannot be said that Janet Keiller invented marmalade, the accidental influx of Seville oranges that wind-tossed day in Dundee influenced her decision to make the distinctive chip-cut style that was to prove so popular. The massive operation her son James set up – the first time marmalade was ever made on such a scale – meant that there were sufficient quantities for it to become a staple of the British breakfast, spreading itself first across Scotland, then across Britain, and finally across the largest empire the world had ever seen.

A Mughal emperor fears chicken bones and a Glasgow bus driver makes a complaint

It's a peculiar thing that, when sifting through 'that great dust heap called "history"', as the politician and author Augustine Birrell put it, we may sometimes come across incidents whose veracity can be counted upon more surely than that of episodes that hail from much more recent times. For example, take the development of one of Britain's favourite dishes.

There are two incidents, divided by a gulf five millennia wide, that are said to have combined to create chicken tikka masala. To visit the first of them, we must go back in time to the early 16th century and the Mughal Empire in south Asia. To eavesdrop on the latter event, so conventional wisdom tells us, we need travel back only as far as 1960s Glasgow.

The tandoor oven was first used in what is now northern India and Pakistan around 5,000 years ago. Made of clay and using charcoal as fuel, it gave food a distinctive flavour. Chicken meat cooked in a tandoor with plenty of spices was a firm favourite five centuries ago in the Mughal Empire, which had expanded to include much of India around 1525. The first emperor, a descendant of Tamerlane called Babur, was a fan of 'tandoori chicken'. What he was not so keen on were chicken bones, which were just the sort of thing that a world leader might choke on and die of (in that respect they were the medieval equivalent of the pretzel that nearly did for George W. Bush). One day Babur sent a command to his cooks that all the bones should be extracted before the chicken was placed in the oven. This could not be done without dividing the meat into much smaller pieces. The new dish of boneless morsels was called *joleh* in Persian, or *tikka* in Punjabi, and quickly became a firm favourite across the Mughal Empire. At some later point, cooks began to marinate the chicken in yoghurt before it was roasted in the tandoor.

Fast-forward to an Indian restaurant in Glasgow sometime in the 1960s. The story goes that a Scottish customer calls the waiter over to complain about his food. His chicken tikka, he cavils, is too dry for his taste. The waiter takes his plate back to the kitchen and in a flash of inspiration – or perhaps annoyance at this philistine's lack of appreciation for the dish – he pours some tomato soup into the sauce. The diner declares himself more than satisfied with the revised version of his order and the rest is history.

One restaurant actually lays claim to being the very locale in which the incident is supposed to have happened. According to one Asif Ali, it occurred not in the '60s but in 1971 at the Shish Mahal in Glasgow, owned by his Pakistani father, Ali Ahmed Aslam. The customer in question was apparently a bus driver, and the proprietor was suffering from a stomach ulcer and was thus eating some Campbell's tomato soup at the time of the complaint. Looking down at his bowl, Ali is said to have suggested that some tomato soup be added to the rejected dish in order to make it more moist. Before long 'chicken tikka masala' ('masala' being a reference to the spicy sauce) was added to the menu as a sop to the British palate.

Regrettably, this is not the sole tale told about the genesis of the dish. Some claim that the tomato had already been added during Britain's occupation of India in order to soften the impact of the spices, to which the colonialists were unaccustomed. Owners of the Karim Hotel in Delhi maintain that the recipe has been known to its chefs since the mid-19th century. The city's famous Moti Mahal restaurant also lays claim to the dish's creation (dating it back to the 1950s). There's also a possibility that the dish is a derivation of a recipe for shahi chicken masala published in London in 1961 in a book entitled *Mrs Balbir Singh's Indian Cookery*.

Whoever has the prior claim to the addition of tomato to the dish, it would seem that the incident at the Shish Mahal was the one that set chicken tikka masala on its way to fame. We can also ascribe the 'tikka' part to one man's fear of death by chicken bone. Since that man single-handedly conquered vast swathes of Indian territory, establishing an empire that would last over 300 years after his death, it's quite impressive that a single order with regard to his cuisine should have made such an impact on modern Britain, where chicken tikka masala now accounts for about 15 per cent of all curries prepared in the land.

Its place in the national diet was affirmed in 2001 by the late Robin Cook, the British foreign secretary of the day. 'Chicken tikka masala is now a true British national dish,' he proclaimed, 'not only because it is the most popular, but because it is a perfect illustration of the way Britain absorbs and adapts external influences.' As Britons become more insular and more opposed to immigration, chicken tikka masala may yet prove to be a perfect illustration of the way we were rather than the way we are.

Mr Bird loves his wife

It is without doubt a discredit to society – or at any rate to English-speaking society – that the word 'uxorious' exists at all. Given the vows of eternal attachment and fidelity that couples exchange when they marry, it seems extraordinary that anglophones have a word that can be defined as describing someone who is excessively fond of his wife, as if there should be defined limits as to how fond one can become before it's all getting out of hand. (It's also revealing that no such word exists to denote someone who is excessively fond of her husband.)

As it is, humanity can be thankful that Gloucestershire-born Alfred Bird not only loved his wife with a passion but also had the wherewithal to improve her life in two very particular areas. The couple lived in Birmingham, where Alfred opened a pharmacy. His wife, Elizabeth, suffered from not one food allergy but two, which was an impressive feat so long before such ailments became *de rigueur*. For a start, she was allergic to eggs, which meant that, among other foodstuffs, she could not eat custard.

Alfred solved the difficulty in 1837 by discovering that cornflour made a perfectly acceptable – if somewhat unlikely – substitute for eggs. He and Elizabeth were the only consumers of his new egg-less custard for some time until they happened to serve the sweet sauce to their friends at a dinner party. Such was the positive reception that Alfred got it into his head to market the product. Alfred Bird and Sons Ltd was established and his egg-free custard powder proved a big hit with customers.

Once Alfred had dealt with the difficulty over custard, he turned all his attention to his wife's other digestive problem: she could not tolerate yeast, which meant that a great many products from the bakery were anathema to her.

Alfred went to work again in an attempt to rectify the situation. It took him several years but eventually, in 1843, when he was still just in his early thirties, he successfully developed a yeast substitute – what we know today as baking powder but which he initially named 'fermenting powder'. Bird's formula was very similar to today's baking powders, which are typically a mixture of sodium bicarbonate and weak acid salts such as mono-calcium phosphate and sodium aluminium sulphate or cream of tartar. When in contact with water, the bicarbonate and the acids react, causing the baking powder to replicate the action of yeast by releasing bubbles of carbon dioxide into whatever substance it's added to (typically dough or batter), thus causing it to expand. Corn starch or potato starch is also added as a preservative, keeping the powder dry until use.

If Elizabeth had not agreed to marry Alfred and he had gone on to live a life of bachelorhood or had contracted nuptials with a woman whose stomach was not averse to yeast or eggs, the world might well be without both baking powder and custard powder and be all the worse for it. The countless delicious recipes that call for baking powder would be lost to us, and custard would be a treat only served when whoever was preparing the pudding could be bothered to whip one up from eggs, milk and sugar.

It's also worth noting that the Birds' son, also called Alfred, took over the business from his father. He went on to create egg-substitute powder, blancmange powder and jelly powder. Although Alfred Jr's three substances were nowhere near as ground-breaking as his father's innovations, they have doubtless brought joy to some quarter or other, the first being particularly useful to vegans.

A nobleman doesn't have the time for a formal dinner

The knack of being in the right place at the right time is something to be envied. In the modern world, it's arguably a gift that is more important than talent and nearly as useful as being well connected or, if you want to be prime minister, going to Eton.

It's fair to say that, on many occasions in his lifetime, John Montagu (who did go to Eton), was in the right place at the right time but was simply the wrong man, particularly when it came to affairs of state. The political life of the 4th Earl of Sandwich is littered with fiascos so dire they would make any modern government minister proud. It culminated in his mismanagement of the fleet while First Lord of the Admiralty, which played a major part in the loss to Britain of its colonies in the United States (though, with hindsight, that may have been no bad thing).

Thankfully for him, he had other arrows in his quiver. He was captain of the Huntingdonshire county cricket team. As sponsor of Captain Cook's second and third voyages, he wound up with a good scattering of islands named in his honour, including two Montague Islands (off Australia and Alaska, respectively, and both with an additional 'e'), the South Sandwich Islands in the southern Atlantic and the Sandwich Islands (now Hawaii). Most memorably, though, he also gave his name to an item of food.

The popular story told about Montagu's association with the sandwich is that he was engaged in an epic game of poker one evening in November 1762. Unable to drag himself from the cards to eat dinner, he is said to have asked a flunky to bring him a piece of meat between two slices of bread – a snack his gambling chums are also said to have eaten quite frequently. If so, presumably their idea was that the bread absorbed the juices of the meat, thus keeping the hands clean for playing and saving the cards themselves from being unwittingly marked by traces of blood or grease.

However, according to Sandwich's biographer, N.A.M. Rodger, it's rather more likely that he made this request to one of his servants while diligently working away at his desk.

John Montagu and (possibly) his gambling circle were by no means the first people to have come up with the idea of using bread as a convenient receptacle for some other ingredient. The Romans were said to be partial to tidbits wrapped in bread, while in the Arabic world, pita breads stuffed with various fillings had been eaten for centuries before Sandwich came along. He wasn't even the first Briton to hit upon the idea of clapping something in sliced bread. In 1748, a courtesan called Fanny Murray, who happened to include the earl among her clientèle, famously took the £20 note she had been given by one Sir Richard Atkins in payment for her services, slipped it between two slices of bread and butter and ate it contemptuously in front of him. Evidently, she had been expecting rather greater compensation for her favours. Since £20 back then is worth about £2,800 today, she may not only have eaten one of the first sandwiches ever made but also the most expensive.

On account of Sandwich's fame – he was appointed First Lord of the Admiralty no fewer than three times – his ways with bread became widely publicised and the 'sandwich' soon caught on both in the *beau monde* as well as the lower rungs of society in Britain and throughout the Empire. Today they habitually form the cornerstone of picnics and packed lunches, there are chain restaurants dedicated to them, and there is barely a corner of the globe where this light meal is not known in some form.

Without the sandwich, there would, of course, be no toasted sandwich-maker. The first one was invented by American Charles Champion in the 1920s and marketed as the Tostwich. However, it was only in the '70s that Australian John O'Brien came up with the toasted sandwich-maker as we know it today, with its clamp action that seals the filling safely within the bread. The company for whom he set up a research and development wing, Breville, has gone on to sell tens of millions of his product. Thanks to him and John Montagu, 4th Earl of Sandwich, people all around the world have the opportunity of biting into a freshly toasted sandwich and squealing in pain as they burn the roof of their mouths off.

Science

God bless scientists. Frequently dismissed by a philistine public as geeky, nerdy and socially inept, they nevertheless push daily at the very boundaries of human knowledge, often without tea breaks. However, on occasion their breakthroughs have owed more to luck than scientific rigour; their successes have hung on a single decision made years beforehand; and the one brilliant discovery that has made their name and brought about a seismic change to society has occurred while they were pursuing something else altogether.

Captain Robert FitzRoy is in need of a dinner companion

Leadership can be a very lonely place – particularly so on board ship. Sea captains, unwilling to confide in or befriend subordinates lest it erode their authority, can find themselves horribly isolated. In the days of sail, when voyages could last months or even years, it could lead to mental breakdowns.

While preparing in the summer of 1831 for a voyage to survey the southern coastline of South America, Captain Robert FitzRoy advertised for a young man to join him as a companion. The successful candidate for the vacancy would take meals with him and in return provide conversation. FitzRoy had taken over his ship when the previous captain – two years into an expedition and aghast at the prospect of mapping the inhospitable coast around Tierra del Fuego – had fallen into a terrible depression, locked himself in his cabin for a fortnight and finally shot himself. Having cast around unsuccessfully for a friend to accompany him, FitzRoy threw the net out wider. The 26-year-old captain was keen to have a naturalist on board: someone who could study the land they encountered while he busied himself with surveying the sea. Therefore, he would only accept applications from gentlemen who were students of natural science. In the great tradition of internships – a tradition perhaps more ardently adhered to today than it has ever been – the position would be unpaid. The ship on which the two-year voyage would be taken was the *HMS Beagle*.

At the behest of his father – a doctor to the great and the good – Charles Darwin had started a degree in medicine at Edinburgh University in 1825. Unfortunately, he found he couldn't stomach the dissections that were essential to his anatomy classes – he would literally run from the dissecting theatre to throw up outside. Thus his father reluctantly allowed him to switch to Plan B: a theology degree at Cambridge followed by a life as a parson. Without ever being inspired by his new subject, Darwin graduated in tenth place out of his class of over 150. More importantly, he fell in love at Cambridge: the object of his passion being insects, and particularly beetles. This brought him into the orbit of botany professor John Stevens Henslow. Having graduated, he had another two terms to spend at the university, and Henslow suggested he study geology under Professor Adam Sedgwick. This latter academic took Darwin on a geology field trip to Wales over the summer of 1831 and opened the 22-year-old's eyes to the importance of scientific theory.

When Darwin returned home, there was a letter from Professor Henslow waiting for him. The missive informed him of FitzRoy's need for a dining companion/naturalist and that he (Henslow) had recommended Darwin for the post. The reluctant parson was jubilant and immediately declared his enthusiasm for the project.

The only difficulty remained Darwin's father, who was most displeased at the prospect of losing his son for two years on what he deemed 'a wild scheme' and 'a useless undertaking' that would prejudice his chances of becoming a clergyman and render him unlikely to want to 'settle down to a steady life hereafter'. Darwin senior told his son he would only be won round if he 'could find any man with common-sense who advises you to go'. Charles appealed to his uncle, Josiah Wedgwood II (of the famous pottery family), whose opinion his father respected. Wedgwood answered his brother-in-law's objections point by point and the paternal consent was duly acquired.

Even so, Charles Darwin still came close to missing out on the voyage, simply because Robert FitzRoy did not like the look of his face. The captain was a devotee of the renowned physiognomist Johann Lavater. In his autobiography, Darwin recalls that FitzRoy very nearly turned him down 'on account of the shape of my nose! ...[He] was convinced that he could judge a man's character by the outline of his features; & he doubted whether anyone with my nose could possess sufficient energy & determination for the voyage.' Thankfully, FitzRoy overcame his doubts and Darwin was recruited for the expedition.

The pair set sail from Plymouth in October. After two false starts, when bad weather forced her to return, the *Beagle* finally made it away across the Atlantic on 27 December 1831. In an unwelcome echo of his days in the dissecting theatre, Darwin was violently seasick for much of the time he was on the water. It was a relief to him, therefore, that FitzRoy was only too happy to allow him to carry out his researches on land while the *Beagle* sailed about surveying the coastline, returning from time to time to pick him up. This was just as well, because rather than the forecast two years, the voyage would end up lasting for nearly five.

The *Beagle* was a little ten-gun brig-sloop, one of about 100 Cherokee-class ships. The design had an unfortunate reputation for being difficult to manœuvre and predisposed to sink – neither of them ideal attributes for an ocean-going vessel. Despite this, FitzRoy successfully sailed her along vast tracts of South America's coastline before heading home via New Zealand and Australia, arriving in the Cornish port of Falmouth on 2 October 1836.

Had FitzRoy preferred to dine alone, Darwin would not have travelled on the *Beagle*. As a result, it's unlikely he would ever have visited the Galapagos Islands. Had that been the case, he would not have been able to study the Galapagos Island finches. He noticed that members of what appeared once to have been a single species of (what he called) finches differed from island to island in one major aspect: their bills seemed to have adapted themselves to take advantage of whatever food was available at each location. In the second edition of his book, *The Voyage of the Beagle*, published in 1845 under the less snappy title *Journal of researches into the natural history and geology of the various countries visited by H.M.S. Beagle, etc.*, he noted:

> Seeing this gradation and diversity of structure in one small, intimately related group of birds, one might really fancy that

from an original paucity of birds in this archipelago, one species had been taken and modified for different ends.

This was the seed that would grow into his theory of 'natural selection'. It posited that organisms that enjoyed advantageous characteristics increased their chances of both surviving and reproducing. These characteristics would therefore have more chance of being passed on to future generations, and thus the species as a whole would evolve over time.

His master work, *On the Origin of the Species*, which he published in 1859, became one of the most important landmarks in scientific endeavour. Inevitably, it also caused a huge scandal for the way it appeared to take much of the work of creation out of the hands of God, and was thus condemned by many as blasphemous. It was for this reason that Darwin (who never became an atheist) had delayed making his theory public for well over a decade, the ideas behind it having crystallised in his mind way back in the 1840s. He was eventually rushed into publication when the naturalist Alfred Russel Wallace sent him a paper in 1858 outlining his own thoughts. Wallace, quite separately, had reached the same conclusions as Darwin about natural selection.

When Darwin took the lessons he had learnt about evolution and applied them to *Homo sapiens* in his 1871 book *The Descent of Man*, the outcry became a howl. For good Bible-believing Christians, the possibility that humans had descended from apes was simply sacrilegious. It's an irony that the *Beagle's* own Captain FitzRoy was himself an ardent believer in the literal truth of the Scriptures and yet his voyage perhaps did more than anything before or since to undermine such a viewpoint.

By the time Charles Darwin died in 1882, his theories had established themselves in the mainstream of scientific life and had been widely accepted by the public. He was afforded a state funeral and buried in Westminster Abbey. And yet, if Captain FitzRoy had not been in need of a dinner companion, Darwin might well have seen out his years as an obscure country parson rather than becoming one of the most influential scientists who ever lived.

A veterinary surgeon cuts up a hose

Anyone who has ridden a bicycle any great distance along a cobblestone street will be able to testify all too readily to the bone-jarring experience that can be. What it must have been like to pedal over the cobbles on a bike with solid wheels can only be winced at. One can certainly sympathise with a young boy valiantly attempting to negotiate the cobblestone streets of 19th-century Belfast on his tricycle.

Fortunately for the young boy – and for millions of cyclists (and then motorists) – his father did not just put an arm around his shoulders and tell him that the experience was character-building, but rather set about to remedy the situation. Since the cobblestones were clearly there to stay, it was the tricycle that needed to be redesigned – or more precisely, its tyres. The boy's father was not an engineer or an inventor but, undaunted, he set to work to find a way of making his son's tricycling less harrowing.

John Dunlop, the father in question, was born on a farm in Dreghorn, Ayrshire, in 1840. Having grown up around animals he became a veterinary surgeon, practising in Edinburgh. He moved to Downpatrick, Ireland, in 1867 and four years later married Margaret Stevenson, with whom he had a daughter and a son. Moving to Belfast, Dunlop built up one of the most successful veterinary practices in the country.

But for one incident in 1887 he would surely have carried on with this perfectly agreeable life and, after his death, his name would have been remembered by no one but grateful animal-owners.

The stories surrounding that event vary but Dunlop either saw his son struggling over the cobblestones or his son asked him if he could do something that would make his ride more comfortable. Either way, he took his boy's tricycle and started experimenting.

His breakthrough came when he cut a length from an old garden hose, looped it around to form a continuous tube, pumped it up and fitted it around a wooden disc. He tested his new creation by rolling it across his yard. He then removed a wheel from his son's tricycle and rolled that across the garden too. He found that the disc with the loop of hose on it went considerably further than the solid wheel. Excited by this turn of events, he fitted tubes to the rear wheels of the tricycle. The effect was immediate and dramatic – the ride over the cobblestones was suddenly a lot less bone-shaking than it had been. John Dunlop had invented the pneumatic tyre. By December 1888 his design had been granted a patent.

Unbeknownst to him, he was not the first person to invent a pneumatic tyre. Just over 40 years beforehand, a fellow Scot called Robert Thompson had patented just such an invention and had registered it in France and the United States. However, the idea had not caught on and Thompson's design had languished in the files of the respective patent offices.

The difference now was that Dunlop's tyre had a sporting champion. Willie Hume, the captain of the Belfast Cruisers Cycling Club, was the first person ever to buy a bicycle with pneumatic tyres. He promptly won all four races at a Queen's College cycling gala in May 1889 with his newfangled tyres, and followed that up with further successes in Liverpool. The president of the Irish Cyclists' Association, Harvey Du Cros, approached Dunlop with the idea of setting up a company to manufacture the tyres, and soon cyclists were taking to them in droves. The pneumatic tyre quickly became a standard feature on all bicycles and the day of the solid wheel was over. The new tyre meant that much greater distances could be travelled in comfort. Cycling boomed.

It's worth noting that the success of Dunlop's tyre was due in no small part to its use of vulcanised rubber. This, too, had come about rather by chance. Back in 1839, in a Massachusetts workshop, Charles Goodyear was experimenting with a mixture of rubber, sulphur and white lead in a bid to create a rubber that would not go brittle in the cold or sticky in the heat. He left his mixture painted onto a patch of fabric and when he returned he discovered that someone had, for reasons unknown, placed it on top of a hot stove. Goodyear noticed that the heat had not made the rubber runny. Before long he had perfected the heating process and vulcanised rubber was born.

The business set up by Dunlop and Du Cros – which they named The Pneumatic Tyre and Booth's Cycle Agency – went from strength to strength, even overcoming the setback of losing the patent rights to the pneumatic tyre on account of Robert Thompson's prior claim. Dunlop did not remain long with the company, and a year later, in 1896, Du Cros sold it to British financier Terah Hooley for £3 million. In the early 20th century, the company was renamed Dunlop Rubber.

By coincidence, Karl Benz produced the world's first motorcar just two years before Dunlop put in for his patent on the pneumatic tyre. A decade or so after the Scotsman's invention had become *de rigueur* for bicycles, a thicker, more durable pneumatic tyre was developed and soon all new cars were provided with them.

Dunlop died in 1921 at the age of 81. He never made a great deal of money from his invention, but his fatherly concern over his son's discomfort resulted in the revolutionising of not just the bicycle but the motorcar as well.

A young artist moves into a derelict Lincolnshire lighthouse

The idea of someone in their late teens or early twenties going off somewhere in order to 'find themselves' has long since become a cliché. In fact, it's become such a cliché that it's a brave person indeed who announces such a plan to their friends without first preparing themselves for the inevitable response of pained expressions and sardonic jokes.

However, back before everyone became so world-weary and cynical – in 1933, to be precise – a young man named Peter Scott took himself off to a remote lighthouse on the Lincolnshire/Norfolk border in order to work out what he wanted to do with his life. The experience was to be transformative to such a degree that a sign posted outside that lighthouse today makes the bold assertion that the structure is, 'The most important building in the history of global conservation…' It also claims that it's the 'most romantic' as well, but that judgment might better be left to the beholder.

Scott was a 24-year-old under more pressure than most to make something of his life. Born in London, his mother was Kathleen Bruce, a renowned sculptor, while his late father had been none other than Scott of the Antarctic, the polar explorer who perished in 1912 during his attempt to reach the South Pole. Peter had been just two years old when his father died. Even so, he found himself growing up beneath the great man's shadow – quite literally so, if he cared to visit his mother's imposing statue of his father that was erected near The Mall just three years after the explorer had met his end. Captain Robert Scott's reputation has taken some blows over the years, but for most of Peter's life he was considered a national hero whose name was a synonym for courage. Even

Peter's godfather was famous, the Scotts having recruited author J. M. Barrie for the rôle. Peter did have the advantage of having a mother who was very well off (donations from the public for the widows of the Scott Expedition members had seen to that), but that may only have increased the expectations placed upon the only child of the national treasure.

Always bright, Scott studied natural sciences at Trinity College, Cambridge before switching to the history of art, graduating in 1931. He had turned out to be not merely a capable painter but one who had the makings of a very fine artist – his talent no doubt inherited from his sculptor mother. He attended the Royal Academy of Art and by 1933 had been offered his first show at a gallery in London. It must have seemed to outsiders that he had set the course for his life. However, Scott felt a sense of unease about his future and cast about for somewhere he could escape to so that he could examine his life in solitude and weigh up his options.

An obsessive wildfowler, Scott had often shot birds at the saltings at Terrington in Norfolk. The flat landscape at the southern end of the Wash was punctured by twin lighthouses built close to the mouth of the River Nene and on either bank. While considering the best place for a bolthole, he remembered these lonely dilapidated buildings three miles out into an enormous tidal marsh. He swiftly rented the one on the eastern bank at £5 per annum and put the proceeds from his London exhibition towards renovation. He added a studio, bathroom, garage and boathouse, and moved in. The decision was to change not only his own life but would also spark a revolution that has shaped wildlife conservation ever since.

The lighthouse had been constructed in 1830 and, despite its name, it never actually bore a light but acted as a customs post and as a beacon to guide ships and boats to the mouth of the Nene. Scott's American friend Paul Gallico visited him there and was inspired by the setting to write the novel *The Snow Goose*, with a thinly disguised Peter Scott as its hero. Gallico described the lighthouse as 'Desolate, utterly lonely and made lonelier by the calls and cries of the wildfowl that make their homes in the marshlands and saltings.'

Ironically, considering the cause to which he eventually decided to dedicate the rest of his life, Scott was drawn to the lighthouse not only because of its remoteness and the opportunities it afforded him to paint, but because it gave him the chance to shoot wild birds.

Scott's deliberations over his future were further complicated by the fact that he was unconscionably gifted at so many pursuits. If a fiction writer ascribed his list of accomplishments to the hero of a novel, readers would find their belief in him stretched well beyond incredulity. Scott was an expert wildfowler and a competition-winning pairs figure skater. In the years ahead he would also win a bronze medal at the 1936 Berlin Olympic Games in the O-Jolle single-handed dinghy competition; race in the America's Cup, taking the helm of the yacht *Sovereign*; and also somehow find time to become the British national gliding champion in 1963. In later life he would show himself a very able writer and television presenter. And then, of course, there was his art.

Living at the lighthouse, he earned a living by selling his work, both at exhibitions and in book form, and it was not long before he achieved a certain amount of fame. His subjects were the birds he encountered on the marshes that had become his world and he found that he derived greater pleasure from painting the birds than from shooting them. As the lighthouse and the abundant avian life around it worked their magic on him, he realised what he wanted to do with his life: become a conservationist.

His aspiration would be curtailed by the outbreak of war in 1939. Scott joined up and served in the navy, rising to lieutenant commander in charge of a squadron of steam gun boats in the English Channel, and winning the Distinguished Service Cross for acts of skill and gallantry at sea. Using his observations of birds he was also involved in the experimental camouflaging of warships, work for which he was awarded the OBE at the tender age of 32.

When Scott was demobilised in 1945 he did not return to the lighthouse. It had been requisitioned during the war and had lost much of its marshland to agriculture as Britain attempted to feed its hungry citizens. Instead, he embarked on the life he had determined for himself while staying there. In 1946 he co-founded the Severn Wildfowl Trust (now known as the Wildfowl and Wetlands Trust) at Slimbridge, in Gloucestershire. Fifteen years later he and a small group of other British naturalists formed the World Wildlife Fund (now the World Wide Fund for Nature), which is now the world's largest conservation organisation. He also designed the famous panda logo for the charity, choosing the animal specifically to entice China into getting involved in the protection of wildlife.

He was influential in forcing a moratorium on commercial whaling upon the International Whaling Commission (whom he derided as 'a butchers' club'), and in the signing of the internationally recognised Antarctic Treaty, which aims to protect the continent as a scientific preserve free from all military activity. While at the International Union for Conservation of Nature and Natural Resources he created what is now known as the Red List of Threatened Species, a globally recognised reference to the world's endangered flora and fauna. He wrote over 20 books and illustrated many others, as well as hosting the popular nature programme *Look* on British television for 26 years. He was knighted in 1973 'for services to conservation and the environment' and died in 1989 at the age of 79.

The lighthouse on the east bank of the Nene still stands, and there are plans to transform it into a centre dedicated to Scott and his work. Had the young wildfowler not happened upon it, there's every chance he might simply have made a career out of his art and ended his days still shooting wildlife. Instead, he is lauded today as one of the most influential conservationists who ever lived.

There's no doubt that his choice would have made his father proud, too. In the last letter Captain Scott ever wrote to his wife, he counselled her to 'make the boy interested in natural history if you can; it is better than games'.

Lord Byron's daughter is taught maths to save her from becoming like her father

The major highlights in the history of the computer are perennially linked with the names of four men: Charles Babbage, Alan Turing, Bill Gates and Steve Jobs. However, it was a young woman who only lived to 36 whose contribution to the invention of the computer, and its eventual evolution into something beyond a mere number-crunching device, was arguably as important as any of these. She is also credited with having written the first-ever computer program way back in 1842, before the first machine recognisable as a computer had even been built. And it all occurred because her mother feared she might be infected by what she considered to be her father's streak of madness.

Augusta Ada Gordon came into the world on 10 December 1815, six months after the Battle of Waterloo. She would be the only child of the three (or possibly four) sired by the poet George Gordon, Lord Byron to be born in wedlock. Her father and mother, Anne Isabella Milbanke (the 11th Baroness Wentworth and known as Annabella), separated a month after Ada's birth. She never saw her father again. Byron became ill and died in 1824 while playing a part in the Greek struggle for independence from the Ottoman Empire. Annabella was bitter about the way she had been treated by her husband, their marriage having lasted for just a year before he had compelled her to leave their home (he had just started an affair and wanted her out of the way). She was also horrified at his sexual escapades – which included an incestuous relationship with his half-sister – and his volatile behaviour. She was determined to bring her daughter up in such a way that she would, in adulthood, exhibit none of her father's flaws: he was 'mad, bad and dangerous to know', to quote Lady Caroline Lamb's famous summation of him.

As a highly intelligent woman who was a particular devotee of mathematics, it was natural for Annabella to cocoon her daughter in a protective programme of maths, logic and science lessons – about as far from the flighty and capricious world of poetry as she could imagine. She employed the best-possible tutors to instruct her daughter, and it must have been a source of great satisfaction to her when Ada started exhibiting a passion for anything that involved engineering. At the age of 12 she would spend her time designing flying machines powered by steam, a full 15 years before such a design was actually patented by William Henson and John Stringfellow. She was also fascinated by scientific journals with their illustrations of the inventions that were helping to power the Industrial Revolution.

In 1835, at the age of 19, she married William King. When her husband was made Earl of Lovelace three years later, she became Lady Augusta Ada King, Countess of Lovelace. She is known today as Ada Lovelace, which is something of a mutilation of the correct form of her name.

However, although her marriage was a happy one that resulted in the birth of three children, an arguably more significant event occurred in her life when she was just 17. In June 1833, she was introduced to a man named Charles Babbage by her mentor, Mary Somerville, herself a very gifted mathematician and astronomer. Babbage, who was 42 at the time of his meeting with Lovelace, was an inventor and the Lucasian Professor of Mathematics at Cambridge University. He and Ada, drawn together by their admiration of each other's mind, soon became firm friends.

Babbage was working on the design of a machine he called a Difference Engine, which would be able to work out logarithms and trigonometric functions. Despite acquiring very generous government funding for his research, he abandoned his attempts to construct such a contraption in order to concentrate on a far more complex device he named the Analytical Engine. On paper, this was the forerunner to the modern-day computer. It contained a component that could carry out calculations; a form of memory; and a means of programming (using punch cards). Unfortunately, it only ever remained on paper – Babbage spent the rest of his life improving the Analytical Engine without ever actually building it. No one – Babbage included – knew the workings of this ever-evolving theoretical machine to such a deep and forensic level than Lovelace.

In 1842, an Italian mathematician called Luigi Menabrea wrote a brief paper based on notes he had taken when Babbage had given a lecture on the Analytical Engine at the University of Turin. Lovelace was asked to translate the paper into English (from French). Since her understanding of the machine was so much deeper than Menabrea's, she ended up correcting a lot of the paper. The following year she shared her work with Babbage. He was thrilled with what he read and asked her to carry on developing it. She promptly wrote twice as much again.

What is most astonishing about the paper Lovelace came up with is just how far ahead of its time it was. She set out in it the first computer programs ever to be published, even though the computer they were intended for had not been built. Indeed, it would not be until 1943, a century later, that the world's first programmable, electronic, digital computer – Bletchley Park's code-breaking Colossus – would see the light of day. Lovelace's programs were not as unsophisticated as one might imagine, either. For instance, one of them would have enabled the Analytical Engine to calculate Bernoulli numbers, a series whose very definition goes way above the head of anyone not deeply immersed in the intricacies of higher mathematics.

Furthermore, while those few scientists who had concerned themselves with such machines had seen them as little more than number-crunching devices, Lovelace predicted that they could be used for a much wider range of applications, including the composition of music 'of any degree of complexity', the generation of graphics and the manipulation of symbols. This last capability is precisely what permits modern computers to carry out enormously complicated calculations. Her paper explains:

> The bounds of arithmetic were however outstepped the moment the idea of applying the cards had occurred, and the Analytical Engine does not occupy common ground with mere "calculating machines". It holds a position wholly its own; and the considerations it suggests are most interesting in their nature. In enabling mechanism to combine together general symbols in successions of unlimited variety and extent, a uniting link is established between the operations of matter and the abstract mental processes of the most abstract branch of mathematical science.

It's a tragedy that one so evidently brilliant died so young. She contracted uterine cancer and spent many months in pain, nursed by her mother, until her death on 27 November 1852 at the age of 36.

In a letter to Michael Faraday, Babbage declared that Ada was '...that Enchantress who has thrown her magical spell around the most abstract of Sciences and has grasped it with a force which few masculine intellects could have exerted over it...'

Although the young Ada clearly also possessed an exceptional natural talent as a mathematician and a logician, because of her sex the conventions of her day would ordinarily have seen these gifts quashed in favour of pursuits deemed more ladylike. Indeed, in the early 1800s it was unusual for girls to receive anything approaching a formal education as we would know it today. The highly exceptional circumstances of her upbringing nurtured and developed that talent.

Nearly a hundred years after she wrote the paper on the Analytical Engine, a mathematician, logician and cryptanalyst called Alan Turing came across it. Lovelace's exploration not only helped shape Turing's ideas on the development of computers but also influenced his work on the cracking of the Enigma Code. As such, one could argue that not only was Ada Lovelace the world's first computer programmer, she also helped the Allies win World War II.

Given her obvious genius and importance in the world of science, it may be difficult to understand why Ada Lovelace isn't a household name. Aside from the usual misogyny that routinely undervalues the achievements of women while exaggerating those of men, Lovelace's reputation has been tarnished because she is her mother's daughter. Annabella Milbanke has been repeatedly smeared by Byron's fans and biographers, who have preferred to view their hero as the victim of the relationship and Annabella as the bitter and scheming wife. Ada simply became guilty by association. 'Lovelace's story is so often printed on paper made from her parents' dirty laundry,' as Suw Charman-Anderson so adroitly put it.

Charman-Anderson is the founder of Ada Lovelace Day, a celebration that occurs on the second Tuesday of October each year. After a century and a half of neglect, it's only right that we should honour the woman who may have been saved from replicating the wild passions of her father, but whose wild passion for mathematics, logic and computers has had such an impact on the modern world.

Three friends take a bet in a coffee house

Casual wagers among male friends tend to home in on the trivialities of human existence. They are usually taken in order to resolve questions that are of no importance to anyone but the gamblers themselves. For example, a bet might arise from a sudden and compelling need to determine which of the assembled company can drink a pint of beer the quickest. Or there's the perennial jousting over whose football/rugby/netball/cricket/hockey/synchronised swimming team will prevail in the coming season, followed by a demand to put one's money where one's mouth is.

Doubtless much the same thing went on in the taverns, inns and coffee houses of London in late 17th-century England. However, it was at one particular coffee house – a famous hang-out for academics and scientists called The Grecian – that three friends cut from a different cloth were about to agree on a wager that would change the face of science forever. The three, all of whom were members of the Royal Society, were Edmond Halley (he of the comet), architect Christopher Wren (of St Paul's fame) and the natural philosopher (i.e. scientist) Robert Hooke.

When a trio with such brilliant minds finds itself in close proximity, the conversation is likely to be highbrow, and indeed the three men were famous for their coffee-house discussions on the scientific and philosophical issues of the day. However, on one occasion in 1684 they managed to outdo even their own lofty standards of erudition, for they ended up laying money on which of them could show the workings for why the path of planets around the Sun was elliptical. In more precise terms, the winner of the wager would be the first of them to produce a mathematical description of the path of an orbiting planet around the Sun if the force of attraction on the planet exerted by the Sun were reciprocal to the square of the distance between them.

It's a problem we've probably all wrestled with ourselves at some point. The difference in this case is that Halley, Wren and Hooke not only had the motivation of the bet to drive them towards an answer, but they also all shared a mistaken belief that no one had managed to come up with one before. It was, they felt, long overdue that someone should, for it had been 75 years since the astronomer Johannes Kepler had shown by observation that the course of Mars around the Sun was elliptical. Beyond that, virtually nothing was known about the path of planets. On account of some work done by Christiaan Huygens on centrifugal force, the three coffee drinkers at The Grecian had a hunch that the answer lay in the relationship between gravity and the square of the distance between the planet and its Sun, and were mustard-keen to set out the maths behind it.

Hooke showed his hand first, claiming that he had come up with the solution, but his workings rather fell apart on closer examination by his two associates. Halley was so energised by the problem that he took himself off to Cambridge – still something of an undertaking in the 1680s – to seek out a certain man at the university who had garnered a name for himself as a mathematician. That man was Isaac Newton.

Newton was 41 years old, a farmer's son from a hamlet in Lincolnshire. He was born prematurely, barely survived his first few months, and was then dumped on his grandmother at the age of three when his mother remarried (his father having died before he was born). It was not an auspicious start in life and he was dogged thereafter by a sense of insecurity. Things turned around when he went to stay with an apothecary while attending the King's School in Grantham. This was his introduction to chemistry, a subject to which the 12-year-old Isaac took immediately and in which he was evidently naturally gifted. Six years later, his uncle, Rev William Ayscough, talked Isaac's mother into letting him study at Cambridge University as he himself had done. Newton was duly granted a place as a subsizar, a student who worked his passage by acting as a waiter and valet for other students.

He continued his studies at the university until 1665, when the Great Plague forced a retreat to Lincolnshire. Newton was not one to let the grass grow under his feet, however. It was there that he formulated his method of infinitesimal calculus and had an apple fall on or near his head – if the legend be true – triggering his 'Eureka!' moment with regard to gravity. He returned to Cambridge in 1667 and two years later became a professor, lecturing on light and its colours, his favourite topic of the moment. His work *Opticks: Or, A Treatise of the Reflections, Refractions, Inflections and Colours of Light* was virulently attacked by one Robert Hooke, sparking a bitter rivalry that would last for years.

By the time of his meeting with Edmond Halley, Newton had gone through a nervous breakdown, not helped by the subsequent death of his mother, which had seen him withdraw from public life for six years. However, during this time Hooke had written to him with the suggestion that the path of planetary orbits might be worked out with a formula that contained inverse squares, an idea that was to resurface in the coffee-house wager.

The story of the encounter between Halley and Newton is recorded by Abraham De Moivre, who heard it from the lips of Newton himself:

> In 1684 Dr Halley came to visit him at Cambridge. After they had been some time together, the Dr asked him what he thought the curve would be that would be described by the planets supposing the force of attraction towards the sun to be reciprocal to the square of their distance from it.

Sir Isaac replied immediately that it would be an ellipse. The Doctor, struck with joy and amazement, asked him how he knew it. Why, saith he, I have calculated it. Whereupon Dr Halley asked him for his calculation without any farther delay. Sir Isaac looked among his papers but could not find it, but he promised him to renew it and then to send it him...

Newton's scientific investigations were somewhat haphazard and sometimes bordered on the eccentric. His fascination with alchemy, for example, often diverted him from what might have been more fruitful avenues of research. However, Halley's visit stung him into action. He sat down and began to lay out a comprehensive solution to the mathematical problem he had been posed. As he worked on it, the scope of his response widened as, for the first time, he set down in a methodical way the ideas he had had over the years on universal gravitation and mechanics.

The first Halley knew of this came three months later in November 1684. A messenger knocked on his door in London and handed him a nine-page exposition entitled *De Motu Corporum In Gyrum (On the Motion of Bodies in Orbit)*. The scientist was gripped by what he read, immediately recognising its importance. He raced back up to Cambridge and cajoled, coaxed and finally convinced Newton that he should expand the treatise into a paper that he could deliver to the Royal Society at the earliest possible opportunity.

Newton abandoned his more arcane pursuits and concentrated on the task Halley had persuaded him to take on. Over the following two years he wrote *Philosophiæ Naturalis Principia Mathematica (The Mathematical Principles of Natural Philosophy)*, a three-volume work of extraordinary genius.

It is at this point, just as this revolutionary masterpiece is delivered to the Royal Society, that the story descends into bathos. The society regretted that it could not publish Mr Newton's work because it was financially embarrassed: all its funds had just been spent on a book about fish that had sunk like a stone.

Although far from being a rich man, Halley immediately stepped in, organising and paying for the publication, an event that took place in 1687. It did not take long for the scientific community to realise that nothing quite like *Principia* (as it is better known today) had been attempted before.

It was a breathtaking achievement: its author had methodically explained the physics behind so much of what happened not only on the Earth, but in the universe beyond.

Among the vast catalogue of achievements in *Principia* are laws which, over 300 years later, are still found to be valid. Its three laws of motion have formed the bedrock for classical mechanics. It also includes an explanation of the behaviour of orbiting celestial bodies; his law of universal gravitation; the reasons for the movements of the tides; and even the evidence for the Earth not being the perfect sphere that scientists of the time believed it to be but a planet that is slightly flattened at both poles. And all of this in Latin.

Principia remains a towering landmark in the scientific landscape, undiminished by the passing years and the advances in the understanding of our universe that have been made since its publication. It formed the groundwork for a revolution in not just one but three realms: physics, mathematics and astronomy. Furthermore, the clarity with which he expressed his ideas set the standard for those who came in his wake. The three volumes – which he updated twice – have been the basis on which scientists have made myriad discoveries of their own, thus shaping our world today. And they simply wouldn't have been written if it hadn't been for a bet that Newton himself didn't even take part in.

It's also intriguing to note that, given the extraordinary scope of *Principia* and its roots in Halley's visit to Newton, nowhere in the pages of the first edition will you find a solution to the problem posed in the Grecian wager. Newton delivers the maths that shows that a planet is subject to the inverse-square force as set out in the bet, but not the maths that describes the ellipsis itself. The author merely states that one follows from the other. Newton later made the claim that he had left out the solution to the problem simply because it was 'very obvious'. If you're a genius, that's the kind of excuse you can get away with.

A naturalist turns down an offer from Captain Cook

One of humanity's most important scientific breakthroughs came about as a result of an invitation to go on a voyage, an offer that was accepted (see page 80). However, it's also true that one of the most important medical breakthroughs in history only came about because an invitation to go on another great voyage was turned down.

Edward Jenner was a 23-year-old surgeon when he was asked to join Captain James Cook's second voyage of discovery in 1772. He had worked on material brought back by Cook from his first voyage and was an obvious choice of naturalist to accompany the great explorer on his next journey. This was supposed to settle the argument once and for all as to whether a vast southern land mass – *Terra Australis* – existed or not. It was a great honour to be asked to take part in such a major expedition, especially one led by such a renowned figure. Along with medicine, natural history was Jenner's abiding passion, and the voyage was the sort of opportunity that would not only expose him to an exciting array of flora and fauna, but it might also make his name. After agonising over his decision, Jenner opted to eschew life as a full-time naturalist to concentrate on making his career in medicine. 'I will decline Captain Cook's offer,' he declared to his tutor and friend John Hunter. 'When I was 13 I chose to be a surgeon, and a surgeon I'll remain.'

He settled down in Berkeley, the small Gloucestershire town where, in 1749, he had entered the world. He was a vicar's son, the penultimate of nine children, and had begun his career in medicine at the age of 14 – a year after his decision to become a surgeon – when he started his seven-year apprenticeship to a surgeon called Daniel Ludlow in the market town of Chipping Sodbury. This was followed by a couple of years of further training at St George's Hospital in London. It was here that he came under the tutelage of John Hunter, a surgeon whose radical medical researches led him to carry out pioneering work in the realm of tooth transplants and venereal diseases.

As Berkeley's resident doctor, Jenner protected the town's inhabitants from the deadly smallpox virus – which killed about one in three of those who caught it and left horribly scarred those who survived – by practising something called variolation. This involved introducing a very small amount of smallpox-infected material into a patient (usually via a superficial scratch) so that they contracted the disease in a mild enough form to survive it. Once they had recovered, they were henceforth inoculated. It was a technique introduced to Britain from Turkey in 1721 by Lady Mary Wortley Montagu and had been used for hundreds of years in China, Sudan and other countries. Closer to home, a survey conducted in 1791 on the island of Easdale, one of the Slate Islands off the west coast of Scotland, found that the community had freed itself of smallpox by employing just such a system of inoculation. However, there was always a danger that too much of the smallpox virus was given to a patient, leading to death or disfigurement.

As a child Jenner himself had been immunised against smallpox by variolation, and although it had successfully kept him from contracting the full-blown disease, it had had a debilitating effect on his health, a state that he suffered right through adulthood. This was no doubt a spur to his experimentation with immunisation. From his apprenticeship in rural Gloucestershire, he had also been well aware of the snippet of country wisdom that decreed that dairymaids did not catch smallpox. It was believed that this was because they routinely caught cowpox from the cows with which they were so often in close proximity. Cowpox is a disease that is relatively harmless to both cows and humans. In the latter, it merely results in a few unsightly pus-filled spots and a short-lived malaise.

However, it was not until 1796 that Jenner hit upon the idea of testing out this bit of folklore to see if there was anything in it. He got his chance when a patient named Sarah Nelmes came to see him. Nelmes was a dairymaid who was worried that some spots (or 'pocks') on her hand might be an early symptom of smallpox. Jenner was able to assure her that it was nothing worse than cowpox (which she had picked up from a cow called Blossom). He then embarked on the sort of experiment that would have medical ethics committees today reaching for their defibrillators. First, he extracted some of the pus from Sarah Nelmes' hand. Then he looked around for someone who had never suffered from smallpox. An eight-year-old by the name of James Phipps – the son of Jenner's gardener – was chosen as a guinea pig.

He made a few light cuts in the boy's arm and introduced some of the pus collected from Sarah Nelmes' hand. Phipps duly contracted cowpox, recovering from it after a week or so. The truly horrifying element of Jenner's experiment was yet to come. He variolated his young subject – exposing him to a small dose of smallpox. He could not be sure of the consequences of such a move after a patient had been infected with cowpox from another person (rather than from a cow, as dairymaids caught it). Thankfully for all concerned, the boy did not take ill and die. In fact he did not take ill at all. Jenner was excited – it appeared that the cowpox had made the boy immune to smallpox. The following year, he submitted his work to the Royal Society but was told that he would need to find more evidence to back his claims.

In 1798, after two years of research during which he had successfully repeated his experiment with a score of other children, including his own baby son, Jenner published a book detailing his findings. Clearly with an eye on the bestseller lists, he gave it the snappy title *An Inquiry into the Causes and Effects of the Variolae Vaccinae; a Disease Discovered in some of the Western Counties of England, Particularly Gloucestershire, and Known by the Name of the Cow Pox.*

In recognition of Jenner's work, his method eventually became known as 'vaccination', a borrowing of the word *vacca* – meaning 'cow' – from Latin. However, the immediate response to his research was far from overwhelming. Indeed, from some quarters it was downright hostile. The anti-vaccination campaigns of our own times – which have been found to be complicit in the resurgence in Britain of childhood diseases such as measles and mumps – are by no means unprecedented. Back in the early 1800s, Jenner's newfangled vaccinations were challenged by those who were, quite understandably, queasy about a disease that came from cows being introduced into their own bloodstream. Others cited what might be viewed as somewhat confused religious reasons for opposing the procedure. The argument went that humans were God's greatest creation, and that cows were not on the same plane, and so it was not right that material that had its genesis in the latter be allowed to taint the former, even if the effects were supposedly beneficial. This line of reasoning didn't explain why it was still apparently morally acceptable for humans to insert much greater quantities of these 'lower creations' into their bodies by drinking the secretions of cows and eating virtually every part of them. (Ironically, Jenner was himself a devout Christian.) When cowpox vaccination was eventually made compulsory by law, protests were organised by those who wanted to retain the freedom not to be immunised.

There were many other reasons why Jenner's book did not start off an immediate revolution in the treatment of smallpox. There was opposition from variolators whose very livelihoods were threatened by his innovation. Furthermore, cross-infection in cowpox doses was sometimes caused by the very people who administered them, since they also came into contact with smallpox sufferers or were treating patients by variolation as well. This could result in people coming down with smallpox immediately after receiving the cowpox vaccine, with the natural lack of confidence in the new practice which that caused.

Jenner valiantly persisted, repeatedly putting forward the case for smallpox vaccination. He worked out more efficient ways of taking pus from the pocks of cowpox sufferers and drying it out so that he could send it off around the world to aid the worldwide struggle against smallpox.

Jenner died of a stroke in 1823, and so never witnessed the immense strides that his methods would take in battling smallpox. It wasn't until 1840 that Parliament outlawed variolation and it would be another 13 years before The Vaccination Act made cowpox vaccination compulsory for every newborn. This act of Parliament was arguably the first official step taken towards the socialisation of medicine in Britain that would ultimately have its apotheosis in the National Health Service. Furthermore, Jenner's discovery of vaccines has provided the foundations on which modern immunology is built.

It took an institution with the global reach of the World Health Organisation (WHO) to secure Jenner's ultimate triumph. A campaign was launched in 1967 with the aim of eradicating smallpox entirely. It was a huge task, given that an estimated 15 million people came down with the disease every year and even the most remote communities were not immune to its grasp. Vaccination programmes were set up in every corner of the planet. It took 12 years but eventually the WHO was able to announce on 26 October 1979 that smallpox had been vanquished.

According to the Jenner Institute, an organisation dedicated to developing innovative vaccines, there are now only two samples of the smallpox virus left in the world, held in laboratories in Siberia and the US and kept under the tightest of security.

Jenner has been fêted all around the globe for his work, both in his lifetime and in the centuries since. Honours and gifts rained down on him from world leaders, including the empress of Russia and Napoléon Bonaparte. Remarkably, as a token of his esteem, Bonaparte released two British non-combatant prisoners of war when Jenner wrote to him requesting such a favour in 1805. Statues of the Gloucestershire doctor have sprung up in cities in all parts of the world, and his former home in Berkeley now hosts a small museum dedicated to his life and work.

Smallpox is the one and only infectious disease ever to have been eradicated by the actions of humans. Captain Cook's loss has very much been humankind's gain. However, it didn't mean that Jenner gave up his natural history research altogether – in fact he was made a fellow of the Royal Society on account of his ornithological work. Cuckoos famously trick other birds into hatching and rearing their offspring, but it was Jenner who was the first to record the fact that a newborn cuckoo, even when still blind, will push any eggs and fledglings out of the nest. By doing so, it secures the full attention of its foster parents and has no rivals for the food they bring to the nest.

Jenner also noticed that the cuckoo is born with a dip in its back that gives it the means to scoop up eggs and chicks. This adaptation disappears by the time the cuckoo is 12 days old. Naturalists were sceptical of Jenner's findings (which, if nothing else, should have prepared him for the reception of his research on vaccinations) until an artist called Jemima Blackburn witnessed the phenomenon herself. When Charles Darwin saw her illustration and description of the newborn cuckoo, it compelled him to make amendments to his groundbreaking work *On the Origin of Species*.

There's a certain delight to be taken from noting that the man whose breakthrough hinged on his taking of a voyage was influenced by the work of a man whose defining moment depended on him *not* taking one.

An English metallurgist aims to improve the rifle

It was Sir Isaac Newton who, in a letter to his fellow scientist Robert Hooke, modestly stated, 'If I have seen further it is by standing on the shoulders of giants.' Pleasingly, even that expression itself was not Newton's own – he was paraphrasing a saying coined by the 12th-century cleric Bernard of Chartres.

In the scientific world, there can have been very few discoveries that did not rely on the work of men and women who had gone before. In the case of metallurgist Harry Brearley, those shoulders belonged to scientists from France, Germany and his native England. However, in a twist on the usual story of one scientist painstakingly building on the work of others, Brearley found himself standing on those giants' shoulders quite by accident. Furthermore – and most unusually for the metaphor – he wasn't alone on the shoulders. In the years immediately prior to the outbreak of World War I there was a plethora of other metallurgists jostling for position with him. They came from Germany, the United States, Poland and (possibly) Sweden, and with one exception (the Swede, whose very existence is questionable), they were all endeavouring to invent the one thing that Harry Brearley came upon by accident. It's true indeed that those whom the gods wish to destroy they first make mad.

Brearley was born in a small and cramped house in Sheffield, South Yorkshire in 1871, the eighth of nine children. He joined the city's Brown Firth Laboratories, becoming its lead researcher in 1908. Four years later, the company was commissioned by a small arms manufacturer to find a solution to a common problem among gunmakers: the erosion of the metal in their weapons. Rifles are so called because of the spiral grooves or 'rifling' on the inside of their barrels. These spin the bullets as they leave the weapon, thus aiding their aerodynamic stability and accuracy. When they are worn away, the rifle loses its effectiveness. If Brearley could come up with a way of slowing down this process, rifles would have a longer life and their owners would be able to kill more sentient beings.

Brearley set to work in his attempts to produce a metal that would withstand the high-speed chafing it received every time a bullet sped along a barrel. It would not be easy. He experimented with metal alloys, adding varying amounts of chromium and carbon to iron to see what would happen. By August 1913, when fortune finally smiled on him, he had racked up a host of failures.

The romantics among us would like to believe that Brearley's discovery – which, it must be said, did not actually help him with the problem he was working on – came about entirely as the myth portrays it. This avers that he was passing a pile of chunks of metal he had discarded as rejects when he happened to notice that one of his previous efforts stood out from the rest. Whilst the vast majority had rusted at the normal rate, this particular one sparkled up at him because it had barely rusted at all. He picked it up and in his hands he knew he had something special: the world's first ever piece of stainless steel.

According to the British Stainless Steel Association, an organisation one would be foolish to gainsay on the topic of its favourite metal alloy, more credibility should be given to other, less thrilling accounts of the discovery. These versions claim:

> It was necessary for Brearley to etch his steels with nitric acid and examine them under a microscope in order to analyse their potential resistance to chemical attack. Brearley found that his new steel resisted these chemical attacks and proceeded to test the sample with other agents, including lemon juice and vinegar. Brearley was astounded to find that his alloys were still highly resistant, and immediately recognised the potential for his steel within the cutlery industry.

The directors at Brown Firth Laboratories were less impressed, especially when the knife blades Brearley made out of his new wonder material simply rusted like any other steel. Thankfully, help was not far away. One of Brearley's friends from his school days, Ernest Stuart, had turned out to be a particularly fine cutler and was a manager at R.F. Mosley's Portland Works in Sheffield. In no time at all Stuart had honed the process by which Brearley's new metal was hardened and 'stainless steel' came into being. (Brearley had actually coined the term 'rustless steel' but Stuart's name for it was the one that prevailed.)

Steel is an alloy of iron and carbon and its discovery dates back to about 200 BC. Stainless steel, by contrast, is a metal that combines iron with at least 10.5 per cent chromium and a very small amount of carbon. This allows the chromium to form an oxidised coating over the surface of the metal, which is what keeps it both rust- and stain-free. Nowadays, silicon manganese is also added, while nickel, molybdenum and other elements may find themselves included in the mix as well.

It's astonishing to consider the number of scientists who came so close to pulling off deliberately what Brearley did accidentally. Nearly a hundred years beforehand there were several metallurgists struggling with the problem of devising an iron that wouldn't rust, but they either didn't use enough chromium or added too much carbon or both. By 1875, a French scientist called Brustlein worked out that, to make a good stainless steel, it was imperative that the carbon content be kept to a minimal level. Two decades later, a German scientist called Hans Goldschmidt developed a process that made that possible. Frenchman Leon Guillet did actually invent a number of alloys which, today, would be considered stainless steel, but he somehow managed to overlook the fact that they were stainless and rustless. Just two years before Brearley's happy accident, two Germans called Monnartz and Borchers noted that there were benefits to having a steel that included at least 10.5 per cent chromium in it. There were many other scientists besides these who had the holy grail of a rustless, stainless steel almost in their grasp and yet failed in their quest to attain it.

That hasn't stopped a range of other people from asserting that they got there before Brearley. The most intriguing of these comes from the German Krupp Iron Works, which maintains that the iron-chrome-nickel hull it made for a yacht in 1908 was in reality the first stainless steel. Unfortunately, the claim cannot be verified because the vessel in question, *The Half Moon*, sank off the coast of Florida. Like a marine-disaster version of Schrödinger's cat, until the yacht is located, its hull exists in two states: pristine and corroded.

The invention of stainless steel handed Sheffield many more decades of prosperity as it churned out countless items of cutlery. It saved the people of Britain from constantly having to polish their steel knives and forks to keep them from rusting. Where its use was adopted in lieu of silver by the upper echelons of society, it also saved their staff from the unending and onerous task of polishing the cutlery in order to maintain its lustre.

Although economic winds (presumably wafted by the vaunted 'unseen hand of the market') have blown out nearly all the furnaces that once gave Sheffield its nickname of the Steel City, there is still plenty of stainless steel being manufactured around the globe: over 40 million tonnes are produced per annum, a figure that has been rising steadily in recent years. The alloy is by no means limited to domestic use either. Stainless steel has been employed to create Newcastle's iconic concert hall The Sage, as well as the Thames Barrier in London, and The Kelpies, a pair of 100-ft tall stainless steel-clad horse-heads – claimed to be the world's largest equine sculptures – created by Andy Scott for the Scottish town of Falkirk.

Perhaps most fittingly, given the urban myth that surrounds its invention, stainless steel plays its own part in another urban myth. It's a widely held belief that the shiny silver-coloured finial on the roof of the Chrysler Building in New York is made of hubcaps. That's not the case – it's just good old stainless steel.

As for a metal that was less susceptible to erosion when used in gun barrels – Brearley never did get around to discovering that.

A chemist standing by his hearth fumbles with a stick

The ability to control fire is one of the features that separates humankind from the rest of our fellow life forms on the planet, along with a desire to mask our own body odour, and a tendency to misspell 'broccoli'.

Although a very primitive pinewood match impregnated with sulphur was possibly in use as far back as the sixth century in China, and would have been on sale when Marco Polo visited in the 1270s, being able to carry around an effective means of producing an instant fire was something of a holy grail for chemists working in Europe. It had taken until the 17th century for them to work out that a mixture of phosphorous and sulphur produced a good fire-starter. The problem with starting one's fire with this compound came in containing it so that you did not set fire to yourself or anything in the vicinity.

Various chemical fire-starters were produced in the early decades of the 19th century. These involved the user embarking on procedures such as dipping sulphur-tipped matches into phosphorous; smashing tiny bulbs of sulphuric acid in order to start a reaction with a phosphorous-headed stick; or other similar courses of action. Aside from being manifestly dangerous, they were also expensive.

Remarkably, it wasn't until 1826 – when the Industrial Revolution was already into its eighth decade, that the problem was solved, and only then because of an accident. The man who had it was John Walker, a chemist from Stockton-on-Tees, a town that was rocketing to fame at the time as one of the termini of the world's first public railway line. The mishap occurred when he was mixing up a potion of chlorate of potash, antimony sulphide, starch and gum.

There is some uncertainty as to the precise nature of the happy accident that brought fire from this concoction. The popular tale is that Walker had stuck a stick into it, presumably to stir the mixture, and was then attempting to clean the stick by wiping it on some rough surface or other when the friction caused it to burst into flames. The truth seems more likely, as reported by the *Gateshead Observer* in 1852 that, 'By the accidental friction on the hearth of a match dipped in the mixture, a light was obtained. The hint was not thrown away.' That article was written 26 years after the event, but it is the closest to a contemporary report we have.

The chemist knew that Fortune had smiled upon him, and by 1827 he had started selling his friction matches under the brand name 'Congreves' (taking the name from a rocket invented by Sir William Congreve). Each box contained 50 cardboard matches and a piece of sandpaper on which they could be struck – all for the price of a shilling.

Matches have been through many more developments since. The use of white phosphorous was supposed to be an improvement on Walker's formula when it was used in place of antimony sulphide, but it had deeply unpleasant side effects, including bone disorders, for those manufacturing them. This led to a strike in 1888 at Bryant and May factories by London 'match girls'.

Shockingly, there had been no need to produce matches using white phosphorous for decades, since the 'safety match' had been invented in 1844 by the Swede Gustav Erik Pasch. He created a match without white phosphorous and had replaced the usual sandpaper supplied for striking a match with a rough surface containing the harmless red phosphorous. The matches themselves would not ignite by ordinary friction or by rubbing against each other, but when the match-head was flicked across the red phosphorous, the chemical reaction combined with the friction ignited a flame. Red phosphorous is still typically used on the striking surface of modern matchboxes.

John Walker, for reasons unknown, did not bother to patent his idea – though, since his matches gained a reputation for sending gobbets of flaming chemicals about the place when struck (leading to bans in France and Germany) it may have been just as well. It did mean, however, that others who came after him were able to improve on his lucky strike, which has culminated in the relatively safe and effective matches we have today.

Politics

Politics may be 'the art of the possible', as German statesman Otto von Bismarck opined, but it's also subject to unpredictable and apparently inconsequential events that make possible the seemingly impossible too. A stroke of luck can prove decisive in setting the country on a new course, while a single misjudgment may change the political landscape entirely.

A young woman misjudges the path of a horse

Ask the woman or man in the street what the defining event of the suffragette movement was – aside from women actually winning the vote in 1928 – and chances are you'll receive a reply along the lines of, 'There was that woman who committed suicide by throwing herself in front of the King's horse.'

And there's no denying that they'd have a point (although many people mistakenly name Emmeline Pankhurst as having carried out the deed) for it caused a sensation at the time and the grainy 14-second film of the incident remains a popular, if ghoulish, view on the internet today. What the clip shows is a stream of horses galloping around Tattenham Corner at Epsom Racecourse on 4 June 1913, Derby Day. After the main field has gone by, a young woman, Emily Wilding Davison, steps out from the crowd, takes a few hurried paces onto the course and turns to face the final five runners. Two pass on the inside of her before she is struck at great speed by the third, Anmer, a racehorse owned by King George V. She tumbles over backwards. Anmer falls, unseating his jockey, Herbert Jones. The horse gets up but Jones lies flat out on the grass. The crowd catches its breath for a second before pouring onto the course, engulfing the two motionless figures.

Anmer finished the Derby jockey-less and went on to compete in several more races. Herbert Jones was mildly concussed but recovered soon afterwards. The 40-year-old Davison was knocked unconscious and died four days later in Epsom Cottage Hospital. She had suffered a fractured skull and other internal injuries.

The story – though horrifying – seems simple enough: Emily Davison, the well known activist with the militant Women's Social and Political Union who had been arrested nine times for crimes that included arson, and who had been force-fed 49 times while on hunger strike in prison, had gone one step further and martyred herself for the cause of women's suffrage, choosing the king's horse to ram home her point.

Scratch below the surface, though, and it appears that this was not really what happened at all. The first problem with the story is that Davison was found to have purchased a return ticket to Epsom. Furthermore, she had made plans to go on holiday with her sister. Neither of these are the actions of a woman intent on ending her life.

So, if she was not trying to commit suicide, the question remains as to what exactly her intentions were that fateful June day.

Evidence has emerged that Davison was one of several suffragettes who, prior to the Derby, had spent some time in a park close to her mother's house, apparently training themselves in the little-practiced art of grabbing at passing horses. The group are then said to have drawn straws to determine which of them would attend the race meeting to put their newly honed skills into action.

When she was taken to the local hospital after the event, Davison was found to be carrying two purple-green-and-white flags. This led to speculation that she had originally been planning to affix one to Anmer somehow, so that the king's horse ran the rest of the race flying the colours of the suffragette movement. An investigation filmed for Channel 4 by sports presenter Clare Balding unearthed the story of a 'Votes for Women' sash that was reputed to have been found on the course after the incident. If it had been dropped by Davison at the moment of impact with Anmer, it would suggest that she had been attempting to slip it around the horse's neck. The sash went up for auction and was donated by the winning bidder to the Houses of Parliament, where it can now be viewed.

In the famous film of the episode, Davison is clearly reaching up with both hands as her chosen horse approaches, though it is impossible to see whether she is holding anything in them, and indeed, it rather appears that she is not. The first British newsreel was broadcast in 1910, so it's somewhat surprising that just three years later, no fewer than three cameras were filming Tattenham Corner that day, catching the collision from different angles. Footage from the other two cameras, though not completely conclusive, does tend to give more support to the sash theory.

It therefore seems more than likely that, rather than attempting to kill herself, Emily Wilding Davison simply misjudged the line the horse was taking. Given the fact that she had just a couple of seconds to position herself correctly in order to throw a sash over the onrushing steed (assuming that was her intention), and this was her first attempt to do so during a proper race, it's not altogether surprising that the tragedy occurred.

Whilst placing a sash over the king's horse would certainly have caused a stir, the death of such a prominent suffragette in such dramatic circumstances did much to help stimulate support for votes for women. This was particularly true among men who, with notable exceptions, had been slow to warm to the cause. Davison's death also led directly to the creation of the Northern Men's Federation for Women's Suffrage, an association formed the same year by the actor Maud Arncliffe-Sennett and which largely drew supporters from Glasgow and Edinburgh.

The campaign was halted for the duration of the Great War, during which the Representation of the People Act 1918 was passed. The Act of Parliament gave the vote to women for the first time in the UK, which in that day included the whole of Ireland. However, it was restricted to those aged 30 or over (men could vote from 21, or 19 if they had seen service in the war) and only then if they were a property owner (or married to one), or if they met one or other obscure criteria, such as being a graduate who lived in a constituency with a university. It wasn't until 1928 that the playing field was levelled and women were granted the same voting rights as men.

It's fitting that Emily Davison has been honoured in the Houses of Parliament, even if it is not for the way she met her end. In order to be able to enter on her 1911 census form that she resided at the House of Commons, she spent the night of 2 April hiding in a cupboard in the chapel of the Palace of Westminster. In 1990, the Labour MP Tony Benn secretly placed a plaque on the cupboard commemorating the incident. The plaque is still there today.

A king's intemperate outburst is taken at face value

English kings have garnered something of a reputation down the ages for not being the most temperate and good-natured examples of humanity. Those who wielded real executive power, unfettered by a counterweight as pesky as a parliament, probably saw it as part of the job description to throw their weight around and generally stomp about armed with a surly, irritable mien. Of course, for centuries it was generally accepted that whoever was monarch had been anointed by God to reign over the nation. It's little wonder, therefore, that kings expected to get their own way and would turn unpleasant if they felt their will was being obstructed, no matter how trifling the impediment might be.

Henry II, the first Plantagenet king, was certainly not known for suffering fools gladly. Coming to the throne in 1154 at the tender age of 21, he inherited a kingdom that had been wracked by the tumult of an 18-year civil war that had only very recently been brought to a close (see page 190). A firm hand was needed if England and Normandy – the lands over which he ruled – were to become strong again and Henry made it plain from day one of his reign that he would brook no opposition in making that happen. However, there was one person with whom he would enjoy very cordial relations: his chancellor and right-hand man, Thomas Becket (the man whom we used to know as Thomas à Becket).

Becket was born in London, probably in 1120. His parents were from Normandy (Caen and Rouen) and had settled in the English capital, where Gilbert Becket had become a wealthy merchant. An intelligent and charming young man, Thomas soon found himself appointed by Henry as the archdeacon of Canterbury on the recommendation of Theobald, Archbishop of Canterbury. He made a success of the post, and the king duly made him his chancellor, an extremely powerful position in the kingdom.

When Theobald died in 1161, Henry took it into his head to make Thomas archbishop of Canterbury, imagining that by this appointment he would control the Church. Becket warned his royal friend that it would not be a good idea to choose him. As head of the Church in England, he explained, he would feel obliged to stand up for the institution even if that meant going against the king's express wishes. Naturally, Henry prevailed and, on 2 June 1162, Thomas Becket was rather reluctantly ordained. Almost overnight the newly fledged archbishop abandoned his somewhat Rabelaisian courtier persona and put on the mantle of the pious and incorruptible clergyman. Indeed, he threw himself so whole-heartedly into the rôle that he gives every appearance of having had a religious conversion. He seems to have become the devout God-fearing individual he supposed an archbishop of Canterbury would have to be.

It did not take long for Becket's prophecy to come true. Two years after taking up his post, things came to a head when Henry called a conference at which he attempted to secularise the judicial system. At the time, England had two types of courts, which were presided over by the State or the Church. The Church courts, which had the right to try allegedly errant clergymen, tended to be a great deal more lenient than those run by the State, with even priests who were rapists and murderers allowed to atone for their crimes by a mere act of penitence. This was an inconsistency Henry wished to abolish by eradicating the Church courts. Becket initially accepted this move but then changed his mind.

The archbishop dug his heels in and found himself summoned to Northampton Castle for a frank exchange of views with Henry's supporters about the matter. Becket quickly realised that, to all intents and purposes, this was a kangaroo court trying him for his refusal to submit to the king's demands. Fearing that he was due to be imprisoned or quietly eliminated, he escaped from the castle while everyone slept and fled with all haste to France, pursued to the coast by the king's envoys. He lived for a couple of years at the Abbey of Pontigny before spending four more at the Abbey of Sens, all the while continuing as Archbishop of Canterbury.

Things might conceivably have continued in this fashion – with Canterbury Cathedral permanently an archbishop short and the English Church (with its massive estates and business interests) trundling along with a perpetually absent leader – until either Henry or Thomas died. However, in May 1170, the hornets' nest was poked again. Henry decided to have his son, Henry the Younger, crowned king, in recognition that he would indeed become king when he (Henry II) died. This was a practice carried out by the Capetians, the dynasty that ruled France from 987 to 1328, and Henry felt it might strengthen his own hand on English soil if an obvious successor had not only been lined up but crowned to boot.

In ordinary circumstances, the ceremony would have been performed by the archbishop of Canterbury. Instead, Henry chose Roger de Pont l'Évêque, Archbishop of York, to do the duties, thus snubbing Becket and, for that matter, putting himself in the wrong with Pope Alexander III as well. It turned out to be a cunning move, for the king had correctly anticipated that the clergyman would be itching to re-crown Henry the Younger himself simply to reassert his rights as Archbishop of Canterbury. Henry met Becket at Fréteval in Normandy in July and offered him the chance to carry out a second coronation ceremony if only he returned to England. The archbishop duly made his way back in December 1170 after a six-year exile. It's fair to say that he felt a certain amount of trepidation about his homecoming, particularly since he was held in contempt by England's powerful barons. (A second crowning of Henry the Younger would eventually take place in 1172, but by then Becket would be long dead.)

With a crushing inevitability, relations between the archbishop and the noblemen deteriorated even further and Becket chose Christmas Day to excommunicate from the Church one Ranulf de Broc and his partisans. It was this action that was to be Becket's undoing. The king had taken himself off to Normandy for Christmas, but news of the excommunication did not take long to reach him.

Posterity has handed down to us several variations of what happened next. What we do know is that Henry became particularly irate and frustrated at this latest turn of events. He lashed out at those around him, somehow forgetting that it was he himself who had chosen Becket as his Archbishop of Canterbury against his erstwhile friend's own advice. He bellowed something to the effect of, 'What sluggards, what cowards have I brought up in my court, who care nothing for their allegiance to their lord?' The exact wording of the next sentence, the one that sealed Thomas Becket's fate, is disputed. It appears to have been on the lines of, 'Have I no friend who will rid me of this upstart priest?' or, 'Will no one rid me of this turbulent priest?' or perhaps, 'Who will rid me of this meddlesome priest?'

Whatever the precise phrasing, four knights who happened to be within earshot clearly felt they understood the king's meaning and rode off for the coast to board a boat to Kent. They entered Canterbury Cathedral on the night of 29 December 1170, just four days after the excommunications had taken place. Becket was standing by the high altar. It appears that initially the knights intended to do no more than arrest the archbishop, but when he did not yield to them and instead clung unto the altar, they set about him, hacking at his head until his skull was split open.

It is often said that Henry II's outburst was in no way intended to intimate that he wanted Becket killed but had arisen from his exasperation with the cleric and was merely rhetorical. To be fair to the monarch, he was a great advocate for the rule of law and the concept of trail by jury, and although he doubtless considered himself above the law, he is unlikely to have wanted his former friend murdered. He certainly repented of his part in the crime afterwards. As soon as he heard of it, he put on sackcloth and ashes, and fasted for three days.

However the king meant his words to be understood, the fallout from them has been dramatic and long-lasting. Ironically, the murder had the effect of making the Church stronger and the king weaker. The people declared Becket a saint, even before the pope managed it (in 1173), and the outrage at the Church courts was washed away by a wave of sympathy. The following year, in a very public show of contrition, Henry walked barefoot to Thomas' shrine at Canterbury Cathedral, allowing himself to be flogged by monks en route.

Canterbury became a major place of pilgrimage, almost on a par with Santiago de Compostela. As a result, the Kentish city became extremely wealthy, with the saint's shrine morphing into a treasure trove of gems and objects made of precious metals. Some historians have posited that, over 350 years later, it was this ostentatious display of wealth that persuaded the perennially acquisitive Henry VIII that there was much to be said for closing down all the monasteries, helping himself to their riches, and setting up the Church of England as a rival to the Catholic Church.

Furthermore, ten months after the killing, Henry took himself off to Ireland (with a reported 400 ships, 500 knights and 4,000 men-at-arms) in a bid to escape some of the opprobrium aimed at him both by his people and the pope. Adding Ireland to his kingdom had always been on Henry's agenda, but the fallout from the murder meant it suddenly became very convenient to start pursuing that end. While he was in the country, several Irish princes came to pledge their loyalty to him at Cashel. So began Britain's long, bloody and bitter involvement in Ireland, which continues today and will doubtless do so until the entire island becomes Irish once more. And almost certainly after that, too.

An MI5 officer forgets to renew his passport

For those people whose work takes them to foreign shores from time to time, forgetting to renew a passport is a minor occupational hazard, albeit one that should only arise once every ten years. When the would-be traveller arrives at the airport, ferry terminal or border only for a customs official to skewer them with a steely glance and a response that starts, 'I'm sorry, sir/madam, but this passport...' one imagines that in most cases the damage is slight: perhaps a meeting will have to be rescheduled or a conference missed. However, it's not the sort of thing one can ever imagine happening to James Bond – or for that matter, a real spy like Mata Hari.

So, when you're a senior MI5 (domestic intelligence agency) officer ordered to fly to France to intercept two suspected spies who appear to be on their way to defect to the other side, turning up at the airport with an out-of-date passport is, in the language one imagines is used nowadays in such circles, suboptimal. When those two turn out to represent a possible 40 per cent of the most notorious spy ring in British history, that little error becomes very suboptimal indeed.

Guy Burgess and Donald Maclean were both signed up as Soviet agents either while studying at Cambridge University in the 1930s or shortly afterwards. They may have been recruited by Trinity College graduate Anthony Blunt or (as Blunt attested later), Burgess may have been approached by a third party (and then recruited Blunt himself). Like the rest of the members of what became known as the Cambridge Spy Ring or the Cambridge

Five, they came from affluent families who moved in rarified social circles.

Burgess was handsome, charming and more than fond of a drink. As a gay man living at a time when homosexuality was illegal in Britain, he had learnt from an early age how to operate below the radar – a skill he would employ to good effect as a spy. He had joined a Tory-supporting society at Trinity College but was influenced by Marxist members of a secret and extremely elitist discussion group at the university called the Cambridge Apostles.

After graduation, Burgess worked as an assistant to a Conservative MP and later as a radio producer at the BBC, where he oversaw *Week in Westminster*, a programme that still airs on Radio 4. In the latter stages of World War II he moved over to the Foreign Office to work in its news department, and after the conflict he became assistant to Labour's minister of state in the Foreign Office. He remained at the government department in various rôles until 1950. During his time there he was able to pass on thousands of documents to his handlers at the Ministry of Internal Affairs, or MVD. This was the Soviet spy agency that had been known as the NKVD from 1934–46 and whose work was assumed by the KGB in 1954.

Meanwhile, Burgess' drinking – which had spiralled out of control – was becoming increasingly problematic for his employers on both sides of the Iron Curtain. He had come close to being sacked from the Foreign Office in 1949 and the following year he was shunted off to the British Embassy in Washington. However, his behaviour continued to be erratic as his alcoholism continued unabated. On 28 February 1951, while on a trip through the state of Virginia, he was stopped no fewer than three times for speeding. Burgess pleaded diplomatic immunity. He had become an embarrassment to the embassy and was sent back to London. There is some debate as to whether he had deliberately sought a way of being posted back to Britain and had engineered this situation, or had merely shown an arrogant disregard for the speed limit that day. Whichever the case, back in London there was an urgent job his Soviet handlers wanted him to carry out.

Twenty years beforehand, Liberal politician's son Donald Maclean had gone up to Cambridge to start his first term at Trinity Hall college. His leftist outlook developed rapidly during his time there and he became well known at the university as a member of the Communist Party. In his final year he was recruited as a Soviet spy by Theodore Maly, a Hungarian-born Roman Catholic priest-turned-Soviet intelligence officer. Maclean was told to give an outward show of disillusionment with Communism and make a career in the Civil Service, where he might prove a useful plant for the newly formed NKVD. He entered the service having passed his exams with first-class honours – his life as a spy had got off to the best possible start.

Like Burgess, he too secured a post at the Foreign Office, where he dealt with the affairs of western European countries and, in 1936, helped scrutinise the policies of the major international players in the Spanish Civil War. The following year, his NKVD contact, Theodore Maly, disappeared (he was probably a victim of the purge Stalin was carrying out at the time) and was replaced by a woman called Kitty Harris, to whom he passed innumerable classified documents.

In 1938, he was promoted to the position of third secretary at the British Embassy in Paris, where he was able to pass on more information to the Soviets regarding the frenetic diplomatic manœuvres Britain was carrying out in the lead-up to World War II. In the French capital he met and married Melinda Marling, the Sorbonne-educated daughter of an American oil executive, and fellow convinced communist. In 1940, the two made a dramatic escape back to England as the Nazi blitzkrieg enveloped northern France. After a period in the Foreign Office, he became second secretary at the British Embassy in Washington, where he was privy to secret information about atomic weapons programmes. He went on to fill an important diplomatic post in Egypt – where he became something of a drunkard – before returning to the Foreign Office in London to lead the American department.

By 1951, the net was closing in on Maclean. US and British security officials had discovered that a dozen coded messages had been sent to Moscow from New York and Washington in the last year of the war by someone code-named Gomer (the Russian spelling of Homer). Maclean was named on a list of nine men who were suspected of being the agent.

Kim Philby, who was later to be revealed as the 'Third Man' of the Cambridge Five, was at the British Embassy in Washington working for MI6 on security matters at the time and was kept informed about the investigations into Gomer. Realising that the agent must be Maclean, he became nervous lest the Foreign Office's American department head be unmasked, an anxiety shared by the Soviets, who feared he might talk and bring other agents down with him. Burgess had just been posted back to Britain after the affair of the speeding offences, and so was instructed to persuade Maclean to pack his bags.

There is some disagreement over whether Burgess intended to defect with Maclean or was tricked into doing so by an MVD keen to pull out not just one but both of their damaged assets. Whichever is the case, Burgess and Maclean planned their flight from Britain and chose Friday 25 May 1951 – Maclean's 38th birthday – as the day on which to do it. Maclean was due to be interviewed by MI5 officers on the following Monday. The encounter might well have proved calamitous for the spy ring, and it was imperative that he be got out of the country before it could take place.

On the evening of 25th, Guy Burgess went to the Maclean family home in Tatsfield, Surrey. Donald said goodbye to Melinda, who was eight months pregnant with the couple's fourth child (the first of whom had died shortly after birth). He and Burgess drove to Southampton and boarded a ferry to Saint-Malo in Brittany.

In 2016, a huge raft of documents on the case was made public in a joint release by the Foreign Office and MI5. The files abound with countless redactions and there are still many more that have been held back by the two agencies, but they do at least put some flesh on the bare bones of this particular defection story.

The official line taken by the British authorities (then and now) is that the disappearance of Burgess and Maclean only came to the attention of the security services on 28 May when Maclean failed to turn up for his grilling by MI5. Thanks to the 2016 release, we now know for certain that this was not true. On account of suspicions arising over the Gomer affair, Maclean had been put on a watch list and an immigration officer at Southampton had alerted MI5 as soon as the diplomat had passed through customs at the port.

A state of panic ensued. Dick White, a senior MI5 officer, was immediately given the task of intercepting the two men when they reached Saint-Malo. He rushed home, grabbed his passport, and raced off to Croydon Airport. It was only on arriving that he discovered that his passport had expired. Perhaps nowadays this would lead to a few phone calls being made and things would be smoothed over so that he could board the plane. Back in 1951, rules were rules, even if you claimed to work for MI5 and needed to apprehend a couple of suspected spies. White was denied permission to fly. Both Burgess and Maclean made it safely to the Soviet Union (though it would be another five years before President Khrushchev conceded that they were living there).

As a result of Dick White's unfortunate oversight, MI5 lost the opportunity to interrogate Burgess and Maclean about their activities and, even more importantly, about who else they knew to be spying for the Soviet Union. Kim Philby was thus able to continue working for MI6 (the Secret Intelligence Service), supplying classified information to the Soviets for another 12 years until he too defected in January 1963. Anthony Blunt, who was a third cousin of the Queen Mother and was knighted in 1956 (the honour was later rescinded), had drifted into the genteel rôle of surveyor of the Queen's pictures by 1964. Although suspicions had hung around him for years, he was only definitively exposed as a spy that year, when he was betrayed by a fellow Soviet agent, Michael Straight.

John Cairncross, the fifth member of the Cambridge Five, only came clean about his work as a spy in 1964. There may even have been a 'Sixth Man' – a physicist called Wilfrid Mann, who worked at MI6 and who was named by the author Andrew Lownie in a 2015 book on Burgess. Although known to both Maclean and Burgess, he was never unmasked (if indeed he was an agent for the Soviets).

A spy ring whose true scope and membership may never be fully known, and whose activities proved exceptionally damaging both to Britain and the US, could have been broken up in 1951. Instead, it continued unhindered for over a decade longer. Burgess and Maclean settled down in Russia, the latter rather more successfully than the former. Maclean learnt Russian, was elevated to the rank of colonel and worked for the Soviets as an expert on British affairs. He was awarded the Order of the Red Banner of Labour and the Order of Combat. Guy Burgess carried on drinking and died of acute liver failure in a Moscow hospital in 1963 at the age of 52.

The capacity of the old-boy network to forgive one of its own is almost limitless. Dick White, who was a friend of Anthony Blunt, became director-general of MI5 in 1953, a knight in 1955, chief of MI6 in 1956, and a Knight Commander of the Most Distinguished Order of Saint Michael and Saint George in 1960. However, it's unlikely he ever forgot to renew his passport again.

The BBC postpones *Steptoe and Son* and David Coleman has an unlikely interviewee

It was the satirist Juvenal who famously declared that the only two things his fellow Roman citizens longed for were *panem et circenses* – 'bread and circuses'. As long as those in power kept them fed and entertained, he opined, his countrymen would never get around to examining their lives or, the gods forbid, rise up against their emperor. It's a cynical viewpoint but it does perhaps offer a more astute insight into human nature than we would care to admit.

In 21st-century Britain, where a public poll on a television talent show can generate more excitement and passion than a vote in a parliamentary election, the observation seems to have lost none of its relevance. It also lends credence to a rather extraordinary story about a decision that looks likely to have changed the result of the 1964 general election. It involves a would-be prime minister, the director-general of the BBC, and a cup of tea in a kitchen.

In 1947, at the age of 31, Harold Wilson had been drafted into Clement Atlee's Cabinet as president of the Board of Trade, making him the youngest Cabinet minister since William Pitt the Younger. Sixteen years later, after the death of Labour leader Hugh Gaitskell, Wilson was elected to head the party. The Conservatives had been in power since 1951 and the still relatively youthful Wilson was keen to end their reign.

He was aided by the fact that his opponent in the general election of October 1964 was Prime Minister Sir Alec Douglas-Home, an aristocrat rather lacking in charisma who, like Wilson, had taken over the leadership of his party in 1963 (from Sir Harold Macmillan).The Conservatives had also been struck by a series of very public scandals, including the Profumo affair, in which the eponymous member of parliament had been discovered to be in a relationship with a woman – Christine Keeler – who was also entangled with a Russian diplomat.

However, the Tories had successfully styled themselves as the natural party of government and Wilson knew that despite their ill-advised choice of leader and the air of sleaze about them, they would be difficult to beat and that he would need everything to go his way if Labour were to win. Perusing the television schedules for the evening of the general election, he noticed something that filled him with dread. At 8p.m., the BBC was showing a repeat of an episode of *Steptoe and Son*.

Over 50 years later it's difficult to imagine how this could have seemed such a devastating blow to the Labour leader. However, in those halcyon days before the internet, before video recorders, and when there were only three channels to choose from – BBC One, the newly launched BBC Two, and ITV – television programmes could accrue massive ratings. In 1962, the comedy-writing team of Ray Galton and Alan Simpson launched *Steptoe and Son* onto an unsuspecting British public. The tale of two impoverished West London rag-and-bone men, played by Wilfrid Brambell and Harry H. Corbett, was an instant success, frequently drawing 14 million viewers and sometimes up to 20 million. This is all the more remarkable when one considers that the total population was not quite 54 million at the time.

Back in 1964 the polls closed an hour earlier than they do today. In an interview given to the BBC in 1981, Wilson told of his fears that Labour voters might have been sorely tempted not to turn out to cast their vote if the alternative was half an hour in the company of the nation's favourite scrap collectors. 'Polling then ended at 9 o'clock,' he pointed out, 'and a lot of our people – my people – working in Liverpool, long journey out, perhaps then a high tea and so on… It was getting late, especially if they wanted to have a pint first.'

Not one to beat about the bush, Wilson called at the home of Sir Hugh Greene, the director-general of the BBC, in order to discuss the matter over a cup of tea.

Greene gave an interview to the BBC in 1982 explaining what happened next:

> Harold Wilson that evening began by accusing the BBC of plotting against him. I told him that he must really know in his heart of hearts that that was untrue, and unless he withdrew that remark there was no point in our discussing anything – we could just have a drink and that could be that. He did withdraw and we talked about the *Steptoe and Son* problem.
>
> The next day I discussed the matter further with the controller of BBC One and we thought a good idea would be to nudge it from early in the evening until 9 o'clock, when at that time the polls closed. I rang up Harold Wilson and told him about this decision and he said to me he was very grateful – it might make a difference of about 20 seats to him.

As it happened, Labour won 317 of the House of Commons' 630 seats, an extremely narrow victory that gave Wilson the smallest parliamentary majority since Lord Stanley's Conservative win in 1847.

The episode of *Steptoe and Son* that was moved to 9P.M. that night was 'The Bonds That Bind Us' (featuring June Whitfield), in which Albert wins £1,000 on the Premium Bonds. There's a pleasing symmetry in old man Steptoe's windfall and the bonanza that the shifting of the programme by an hour delivered to Harold Wilson. The prime minister was able to call a snap election two years later and increase his majority to nearly 100, securing him a further four years as the leader of the nation (he won a further two from 1974–76).

During those six years, Wilson was socially very liberal, abolishing capital punishment and easing laws on abortion, censorship and homosexuality, while bringing in laws to help in the fight against discrimination on the grounds of sex or race. He kept Britain out of the Vietnam War but was forced to devalue the pound. He also applied for membership of the European Economic Community (EEC) but was turned down. Under his premiership Britain also saw the expansion of higher education, including the establishment of the Open University which the Wilson government legislated for (it opened in 1971, by which time Labour had been swept from power). Its model of teaching has been imitated all over the world.

It's worth noting that, to a great extent, Harold Wilson's undoing in the 1970 general election can be laid at the door of another television show that also had nothing to do with politics. When the deeply unpopular leader of the Conservative Party, Edward Heath, won the Sydney-to-Hobart yacht race in December 1969, he was interviewed by David Coleman on a programme called *Sportsnight*.

The appearance suddenly showed Heath in a completely new light – until then he had been generally viewed by the public as a posh, stiff and emotionless man who was hopelessly out of touch with the concerns of the average Briton. Although he doubtless remained all of these things, his new image as a successful sportsman gave the party a more appealing veneer, and Wilson – who was reportedly angered by his opponent's *Sportsnight* slot – crashed to unexpected defeat at the polls just six months later.

As a result of Heath's win, Britain experienced the miners' strikes of 1972 and 1974 and the consequent three-day week caused by electricity rationing. An ardent Europhile, Heath succeeded where Wilson had failed, signing the treaty of accession that sealed the

UK's entry into the EEC on 1 January 1973. He also introduced Value Added Tax (VAT). This quickly became the Conservative Party's stealth tax of choice, with subsequent Tory governments raising it from Heath's initial 10 per cent on most products (some were subject to a higher rate) to 15 per cent, 17.5 per cent and now to 20 per cent. This, one of the most enduring elements of Heath's legacy (even more enduring than Britain's membership of the European single market, it would seem), affects the life of every Briton pretty much daily, particularly those at the poorer end of society who spend a greater percentage of their income on goods that attract VAT.

As such, *Sportsnight* can perhaps make a greater claim to changing the political face of the nation than many a television programme dedicated to politics.

But we should leave the last word to Harold Wilson and *Steptoe and Son*. In Wilson's 1981 interview, he recalled his meeting with Sir Hugh Greene:

> I said I didn't want a popular programme between 8 and 9 o'clock. It was the equivalent of bringing Morecambe and Wise back. Hugh didn't think much of this argument. He said what would you prefer to put on between 8 o'clock and 9 o'clock? I said, "Greek drama, preferably in the original."

It would have been highly appropriate had the BBC filled the slot with such a play: a module on Greek drama is offered at Wilson's Open University today.

A former colonel rides his motorbike through a dip in the road

Lawrence of Arabia. Utter the name and suddenly visions arise of Peter O'Toole in David Lean's classic Oscar-winning film, ice-blue eyes heroically scanning the horizon as he rides a camel through the desert. A swashbuckling hero with a devil-may-care attitude, Lawrence had reserves of courage that would shame most other mortals. If even half the stories about him are true, he was a man who lived an extraordinary life, the effects of which are still felt today. That his death should also have made its mark should not, therefore, be a surprise. That it was an entirely unwitting legacy Lawrence was to pass on to future generations, and one that he would doubtless have poured scorn on himself, is one of those odd quirks of fate that make the world such an appealingly unpredictable place in which to live.

He was born Thomas Edward Lawrence in Tremadog, Wales, on 16 August 1888. His mother was Sarah Junner, a Scottish governess, and his father was Sir Thomas Chapman, an Anglo-Irish nobleman who had abandoned his first family in Ireland to live with Junner. The surname Lawrence was entirely fictitious – the couple had assumed it to cover the fact that they were not married and then, quite naturally, had passed it on to their son in order to keep up the pretence. It was an unconventional start to an unconventional life.

Lawrence gained a place at Oxford University to read history and headed off to the Middle East in 1910 as an archaeologist, digging mainly in areas that are today part of Syria. It was World War I that was to make his name as well as his nickname. Using his brilliant leadership and language skills and, just as importantly, his knowledge and respect for the Arab people and their culture, he led a guerrilla force composed of Arab fighters against the might of the Ottoman Empire, eventually helping to capture Damascus. He ended the war a colonel.

A short while later he returned to Oxford to begin a fellowship at All Souls College and the writing of his best-selling war memoir, *Seven Pillars of Wisdom*. He also served as a diplomat but found the widespread acclaim for his rôle in the Great War difficult to live with; in 1922 he deliberately attempted to disappear from public view. He spent the remaining 13 years of his life striving – largely in vain – to achieve obscurity. He enlisted in the Royal Air Force as a lowly aircraftman under the name John Hume Ross and served a short time as a private in the army as T. E. Shaw before returning to the RAF.

While he may have endeavoured to avoid the unwanted trappings of his fame, the daredevil streak in him did not go away. He was a collector of Brough motorcycles and a lover of the high speeds (in excess of 100mph) they could attain, writing once that, 'A skittish motor-bike with a touch of blood in it is better than all the riding animals on earth.'

It is not known whether Lawrence was travelling at any undue velocity on his Brough Superior 1100 on the morning of Monday 13 May 1935. What we do know is that it was raining very hard and that a dip in the road near his Dorset home restricted the view of what lay up ahead of him. It meant that he did not see two boys on bicycles until it was too late. He swerved to avoid them but lost control of his machine and was thrown over the handlebars. The damage he sustained to his head when it hit the road was severe, and despite the best efforts of hospital doctors, he died six days later. He was 46. Like most motorcyclists of his time, Lawrence was not wearing a crash helmet.

One of the doctors who had fought to save his life was a man named Hugh Cairns. The young neurosurgeon – one of the first in Britain – was deeply affected by Lawrence's death. He grew absorbed by the problem of head traumas suffered by the victims of motorbike accidents and wanted to find out to what extent crash helmets prevented them. It seems an all-too-obvious line of thought to pursue now, but back in the 1930s such notions were groundbreaking.

He had his first report published in the *British Medical Journal* in 1941 while serving in the army. It contained the shocking statistic that in the 21 months leading up to the outbreak of World War II, 1,884 motorcyclists had perished on Britain's roads, two-thirds of them as a result of head injuries. With the advent of blackouts during the war, the death toll rose even higher, to between three and four every day. While crash helmets could never bring this horrifying total down to zero, Cairns' investigations convinced him that they would at least reduce the casualties.

By November, Cairns' work had persuaded the army top brass to issue an order that henceforth all despatch riders should wear a helmet. By the end of the war, death from accidents among army motorcyclists had fallen by around 75 per cent.

Despite the overwhelming evidence that Cairns had compiled to show that the wearing of crash helmet made the motorcyclist much less likely to die in a crash that involved a blow to the head, it wasn't until 1973 that legislation was introduced in Britain making their use compulsory. There had been a good deal of opposition from those who saw their imposition as an infringement of personal freedom, but the counter-argument won the day. The law paved the way for another major piece of road-safety legislation ten years later – the compulsory use of seat belts by those in the front of cars (back-seat passengers were also obliged to belt up by 1991).

In his relative short span on Earth, Lawrence demonstrated both figuratively and literally that he did not have a 'crash helmet' approach to life. It's an irony, therefore, that his death brought about legislation that forced his fellow motorcyclists to adopt a measure that would contribute considerably to their safety, but which one can hardly imagine Lawrence adopting himself.

Motorcycle usage in Britain, in terms of miles ridden, is slightly higher nowadays than it was in 1973, when helmets became compulsory. Despite that, fatalities among motorcyclists have fallen from over 700 that year to 331 in 2013. The drop in serious injuries to bikers resulting in accidents on the road has been even more acute. Naturally, not all of this can be put down to the use of crash helmets, but the statistics tend to support the idea that their adoption has saved the lives of thousands of riders and kept many more from sustaining severe head injuries. And all because there was a dip in the road near Lawrence of Arabia's Dorset home.

An elderly Burmese woman falls dangerously ill just before a national uprising

It is 1988 and in the then Burmese capital of Rangoon, Khin Kyi's health has deteriorated badly. The 76-year-old is the widow of General Aung San, a hero of the struggle for Burmese independence and a de facto prime minister of British Burma who had been assassinated in 1947. She is also the mother of four children, two of whom died very young. Her only daughter lives abroad, as she has done most of her life. After schooling in India, where Khin Kyi was Burmese Ambassador, her daughter had gone to Oxford University where she graduated in philosophy, politics and economics. After a spell in the United States working at the United Nations, she had married an Englishman and had eventually settled down in England, where she had given birth to two children of her own and written several books.

When Aung San Suu Kyi received word of her mother's illness, she had no designs on becoming an internationally recognised political figure, and certainly had no desire to become one of the world's most famous prisoners. She rushed to her mother's bedside. While she was caring for her, Burma's military leader General Ne Win resigned after 26 years at the helm amidst a mass popular uprising in 1988. This was put down by the country's widely despised junta, resulting in the deaths of thousands of protesters. Just a week later, Suu Kyi wrote an open letter to the government, calling upon it to hold free multi-party elections. Well known in Burma on account of her parents, she made her maiden public speech soon afterwards to an immense crowd outside the Shwedagon Pagoda.

By September she had founded the National League for Democracy (NLD). Her mother died in December. The following year, the military government declared that Burma would be known as Myanmar (a name that many Burmese refuse to recognise).

Suu Kyi's demand for elections was eventually granted – the military junta had reckoned that the dizzying number of parties contesting votes would ensure that no clear result was possible and they would be able to use this as an excuse to remain in power. They also banned Suu Kyi from standing for election, though this did not deter her from campaigning on behalf of her party. Come July 1989, her popularity was so great that the military rulers had her placed under house arrest, though without bringing charges against her or sending her to trial. The following year, the delayed elections took place and the NLD won an astonishing 80 per cent of all the seats in parliament. Naturally enough, the junta refused to recognise the result.

Over the 21 years from her first arrest, Suu Kyi was to be imprisoned for 15 years, almost all of that time under house arrest charged with spurious crimes or none at all. She also spent over three months in secret detention. She was released twice, only to be arrested again, before being freed for the final time in 2010, six days after an election in which the NLD had refused to run because of changes to the electoral laws specifically designed to damage the party. During her prolonged periods of confinement there were numerous calls from the United Nations for Suu Kyi's release. These were simply ignored by the junta. She also won the Nobel Peace Prize in 1991 while under house arrest, and the Congressional Gold Medal in 2008, making her the first person ever to win the US government award while imprisoned.

The most affecting detail of what must have seemed to Suu Kyi two interminably long decades was that her husband, Michael Aris, was almost never allowed to visit her from Britain. The last time the two saw each other was at Christmas 1995, during a period when Suu Kyi was not under house arrest. When Aris was diagnosed with prostate cancer, he asked the Burmese authorities if he could come to Burma one last time in order to say goodbye. The request was refused. Instead, Suu Kyi was encouraged by the junta to leave Burma in order to visit him. Believing that she would not be allowed to re-enter the country if she did so, she stayed put. Aris died in March 1999.

Suu Kyi made a successful bid for election to parliament in 2012. Three years later, the electorate delivered a landslide victory to her NLD party, giving them 390 of the 498 seats that the military allowed to be contested. In 2016, the NLD chose Htin Kyaw as president of Burma. As leader of the NLD, Suu Kyi should have become president, but a cynical change to the constitution put in place by the junta in 2010 barred anyone who had ever been married to a foreign national from holding that office. However, a few months later, the party created the post of 'state counsellor' for her and Suu Kyi has since declared that she will rule 'above the president' until such a time as the constitution can be changed.

Not everything has gone perfectly since the NLD took over the reins of government. In 2017, Suu Kyi had to answer questions about the alleged ethnic cleansing of the Rohingya Muslim minority in Burma and accusations that the army was carrying out atrocities in operations against ethnic insurgent groups (under the current constitution, the army is not under the control of the government).

However, had Khin Kyi not fallen ill just before the uprising, there's every chance that her British-based daughter, bringing up British-born children, would not have become so enmeshed in her country's fight for democracy, nor would she have become the figurehead for it. Without her and the perseverance of her party, the generals might still be ruling Burma today. Instead, Burma is a democracy once more and has a government concerned with rebuilding the country by investing in its infrastructure, creating jobs and improving health care. One can only imagine that both Suu Kyi's parents would have been immensely proud of that.

It's also fitting that Britain, which ruled Burma from 1824–1948 (albeit with a major incursion by the Japanese during World War II), and whose colonisation of the country helped sow the seeds of the long military dictatorship that Burma suffered, should play a small part in the restoration of democracy there.

A cyberspace prank is played on Prince Philip before the internet even exists

'Ah yes, this is an idea whose time has come,' we purr, as we gaze down at the self-propelling hummus dish. 'If only every innovation arrived at precisely the hour it were required.'

It's indeed a sad fact that history is littered with ideas that are simply too far ahead of their time to succeed. In the 15th century, Leonardo da Vinci was drawing plans for helicopters, a form of transport that would only become reality in the 20th century. René Descartes' 1636 dream of a contact lens only became reality in 1888. And then there is Prestel.

Almost forgotten now, Prestel was Britain's very own internet before the internet itself came on the scene. Launched by the Post Office in 1979, it was an information network that anyone could access from their home or business if they had a phone, a modem, a computer and a television (to use as a monitor). Invented by research engineer Sam Fedida, it was initially called Viewdata, marketed under the brand name Prestel, and used the phone network to link databanks brimming with useful information – a cool 100,000 pages at its launch, covering news, sport, transport timetables and a whole range of other areas.

Unfortunately, very few Britons were impressed by this. As 1981 dawned, Prestel had a mere 6,000 customers. Undaunted, the Post Office expanded the system. Unlike Teletext, Prestel was interactive – it began to offer online banking services for

Bank of Scotland and Nottingham Building Society customers, theatre-ticket booking, and online shopping. A service called Micronet 800 allowed Prestel users to participate in chat rooms and online games. Another Micronet innovation called Mailbox gave users the chance to send messages to one another.

It was this last service that grabbed the attention of two British journalists – Robert Schifreen and Steve Gold. One day in October 1984, Schifreen was testing a modem when he found that some random numbers he had typed had gained him entry onto a page used by Prestel's administrators (by that time British Telecom had taken over from the Post Office). This later gave him access to login information that allowed him to hack into the system.

Disturbed by the slipshod nature of Prestel's security, which had been called into question repeatedly by other users and computer experts, Schifreen decided to have a look into Prince Philip's Mailbox account. He would then publicise what he had done, and in this way compel British Telecom to do something about its approach to security.

In an interview with John Leyden for the online tech magazine The Register, Schifreen said that after he had had a browse around the royal inbox, 'I phoned Steve [Gold] (who'd been pursuing Prestel in other ways). I then went and told Micronet what I'd done, and they told Prestel... who called in the Met [Metropolitan Police].'

Schifreen is leaving out a couple of the rungs in the ladder there. As Prestel was being told of the breach, Gold and Schifreen broke the story in the press, which meant that it got picked up by the national television news networks. Margaret Thatcher, who was in the process of ensuring that as much of Britain's infrastructure was owned by as few Britons as possible, was beside herself with fury at the story, fearing that it might damage British Telecom's forthcoming sell-off.

The prime minister, never one burdened with the need to fool people into thinking she didn't know the price of everything and the value of nothing, pressurised Prestel into reporting the whistle-blowing pair to the police.

Both Schifreen and Gold were arrested. Farcically, since no legislation existed that specifically covered computer crime, they had to be charged under Section 1 of the Forgery and Counterfeiting Act 1981. The 'forgery' supposedly involved was somewhat tenuous. The prosecution applied it to the use of a password to enter the system and the damage caused afterwards (to prove he had gained access, Schifreen made a very minor change on the master page).

The two men pleaded 'not guilty' at the Crown Court on the grounds that they had not broken any law. When they were found guilty, they took their case to the Court of Appeal and won. The Crown responded by appealing to the House of Lords, which likewise found in favour of the defendants, on the grounds that the 'forgery' had only existed for a minute fraction of a second.

Although there had been previous computer-related cases that had been tried by contorting existing legislation, the Schifreen and Gold case exposed the glaring inadequacy of the law when it came to computer crime. The result was the Computer Misuse Act of 1990. Although it, too, was far from perfect, it was used by other countries as a template for their own laws that attempted to deal with computer-related offences. The British version has been updated several times since in a bid to keep up both with computer technology and evolutions in the development of the internet.

Ultimately, Prestel proved too expensive for its users, who were unwilling to fork out the £20 per annum subscription on top of usage charges and any equipment they might need to buy to get themselves online. The service kept going until 1994, when it was sold off and petered out, cruelly brushed aside by the emerging internet and its sparkly new World Wide Web. However, at least its administrators can claim the dubious honour of practising security procedures so lax that they sparked off a whole new field of British law.

As for Prince Philip's mailbox, which had been at the centre of the maelstrom, the contents amounted to little more than messages from Prestel users sending good wishes to Princess Diana on her birthday. Those were more innocent times.

Music & Literature

In an ideal world, musicians and (particularly) authors would be the most revered members of our society. Their output has shaped the culture we live in and given us countless hours of enjoyment, making life itself worth living. However, some of the most influential and best-loved works of music and literature might never have come into being had it not been for a serendipitous episode, while other little-known events have had repercussions far beyond their import at the time.

A mender of kettles refuses to leave prison

'Necessity,' we're told, 'is the mother of invention.' 'Brevity,' Shakespeare claimed, 'is the soul of wit.' If these thoughts were two wise monkeys, one might say that the third could be, 'Adversity is the wellspring of creativeness.'

In the case of a certain 17th-century pot-mender-turned-itinerant-preacher, the fact that he rather brought the adversity upon himself doesn't seem to have in any way dimmed the fire of artistic expression. He was initially imprisoned for six months for preaching without a licence. However, it was only his repeated stubborn refusals to give his word that he would not continue preaching once he was free again that meant this relatively brief sentence eventually turned into a 12-year stretch.

Had he not been subjected to this lengthy prison term the world would have been deprived of one of its most enduring works of literature. The book the recalcitrant preacher wrote in his cell has never been out of print since its publication over 300 years ago and has become the best-selling work of fiction ever written.

If one had been at his mother's bedside as she gave birth to little John Bunyan, it would have been difficult to imagine that much would come of the new life brought forth. The little mite was born into poverty in a Bedfordshire village called Elstow in 1628. His living conditions as a child were far from ideal: 'My father's house being of that rank that is meanest and most despised of all the families in the land,' as he was later to recall. However, his mother had come from a family of marginally higher social standing than her husband's, which probably explains how she somehow managed to send little John to school. If nothing else, this meant at least that her son learnt to read.

The English Civil War (or the War of the Three Kingdoms, as historians prefer to call it nowadays, since it spread beyond England's borders) broke out when Bunyan was a teenager, and at 16 he signed up for military service, spending the next three years in the army. Somewhat farcically, until relatively recently no one was at all sure whether he'd fought for the king or for Parliament. Bunyan himself didn't see fit to record with which side he had fought, not even deigning to point it out in his autobiography. It wasn't until some Civil War muster rolls were discovered at Newport Pagnell, where he was stationed, that it was determined that Bunyan had been a Roundhead, serving under the command of Sir Samuel Luke. Almost nothing is known about the actions Bunyan took part in, though he may have been involved in the siege of Leicester.

Soon after leaving the army Bunyan married. We know next to nothing about his wife – not even her name – aside from the fact that she was as poverty-stricken as her husband, 'not having so much household stuff as a dish or a spoon betwixt us both' as Bunyan noted. However, she did own two books, *The Plain Man's Pathway to Heaven* and *The Practice of Piety*. Bunyan the kettle-mender had, by this point, more or less forgotten how to read, so his wife had to rekindle his literacy skills using these two books. It was on account of them that he underwent a spiritual civil war of his own, doubting the Christian message but still ineluctably drawn to it. It was a struggle that went on for several years.

It was when he came under the wing of the minister of a Puritan group in Bedford, one John Gifford, that Bunyan was at last drawn into the Church. He moved his family to Bedford from Elstow (which was only a mile away) and after a couple of years became a deacon at the church. He began preaching at nearby villages and towns, a course of action that would eventually be both his undoing and his making.

Bunyan did not possess the requisite licence to preach. He was first charged in 1658 but the case doesn't appear to have made it to court. Bunyan continued preaching and began writing pamphlets, initially attacking Quakers, whom he regarded as folk who did not take the Bible seriously enough. His last work before the storm really broke over him was the eye-catchingly titled *A Few Sighs from Hell, or the Groans of a Damned Soul; by that poor and contemptible servant of Jesus Christ, John Bunyan*.

It was one of those tragic 'Ah, if only they hadn't done that' events in British history that was to curtail Bunyan's freedom. In 1660 the monarchy was restored. Despite assurances given by the perfidious Charles II prior to his coronation, laws aimed against members of non-conformist churches were re-enacted.

It was unfortunate for Bunyan that the magistrates at the quarter sessions in Bedford were particularly zealous in cracking down on those who dared stray outside the Church of England. One of them, Sir Francis Wingate, heard that Bunyan was to undertake a preaching engagement near the village of Lower Samsall, and made haste to have him arrested. Bunyan got wind of this and could have fled, but reckoned that it was his moral duty to preach until he was stopped: an attitude that has afflicted many a preacher since.

Wingate didn't really have anything substantial with which to charge the preacher, but he sent him to Bedford Jail anyway in order to give himself time to dig up some dusty forgotten law he could use against him at the next quarter sessions. Sure enough, two months later, in January 1661, Bunyan was charged under the obscure Conventicle Act of 1593, which parliamentarians had forgotten to repeal. The pot-mender from Elstow was found guilty of 'perniciously abstaining from coming to church to hear divine service, and for being a common upholder of several unlawful meetings and conventicles to the great disturbance and distraction of the good subjects of this kingdom'.

He was given a three-month sentence. However, there was a catch: if after that he did not agree to go back to church (by which was meant a Church of England church, of course) and stop preaching, he faced being exiled. If that occurred and he dared to come back into Britain, he would be hanged. Despite these rather draconian measures, when Bunyan's three months were up he simply refused to give the undertakings his accusers sought. Rather than deporting him, they kept him in prison. And all the while Bunyan refused to stop preaching, he remained there. He believed it was the will of God that he should give sermons and so he told magistrates that he would rather stay in prison until moss grew on his eyelids than be free and not preach. Although he was actually let out for brief periods – to spend a night at home or, on one occasion, make a trip to London – his three-month sentence would end up lasting 12 years.

The upside to this enforced hiatus in his life was that it allowed him to devote much more time to his writing. There is disagreement among historians as to whether his greatest work was penned at this time or during a later imprisonment that he suffered, but the available evidence favours this former period of incarceration. Indeed, some Bunyan scholars have posited that the final six years of this confinement were dedicated to the writing of the book – *The Pilgrim's Progress* – that would make his name.

Bunyan's religious allegory follows the journey of a man named Christian from the City of Destruction to the Celestial City. On the way he passes through such places as the Slough of Despond, the Hill of Difficulty, the Valley of the Shadow of Death, Vanity Fair, and the River of Death. Christian carries a great burden on his back (representing sin) and meets with a cavalcade of contrasting characters: Obstinate, Mr Worldly Wiseman, Goodwill, Hypocrisy, Faithful, Ignorance, Mr Ready-to-Halt, Mr Great-Heart and a host of others. As their names suggest, some are helpful to him while others are a distraction or a danger.

The story is also noteworthy for its inclusion of a giant called Pope who lives in a cave (with fellow giant Pagan) in the Valley of the Shadow of Death and is portrayed as a doddery old man 'grinning at Pilgrims as they go by, and biting his nails, because he cannot come at them'.

The book was a huge hit from the moment of publication in 1678. By 1692 it had sold over 100,000 copies – a colossal number for the period. It was said that every English household had its Bible and its *Pilgrim's Progress*. Bunyan's allegory went on to become the second highest selling book in publishing history, surpassed only by the Bible. Its virulently anti-Papist message helped normalise ill-feeling towards Catholics in Britain, an attitude that saw its culmination in the Glorious Revolution, in which the Catholic James II was replaced by the Protestant William and Mary.

The Pilgrim's Progress also proved highly influential abroad: Christian missionaries sailing out from Britain carried copies of it with them to use as a simple evangelistic tool. It has now been translated into more than 200 languages.

The book has left its mark in others ways, too – its influence can be seen very explicitly in many of the great works of English literature such as Louisa May Alcott's *Little Women*, William Makepeace Thackeray's *Vanity Fair*, Charlotte Brontë's *Jane Eyre* and John Steinbeck's *The Grapes of Wrath*, among many others. Ralph Vaughan Williams wrote an opera based on the story for the 1951 Festival of Britain, and several film directors have had a stab at recreating it on the big screen, with the first attempt reaching cinemas as early as 1912.

Bunyan was released in 1672 – when all laws targeting non-conformists were suspended – only to be imprisoned again three years later when the political winds changed. On that occasion, though, he was only held for six months, probably in a one-cell jail on a bridge crossing the River Ouse. He spent his last years in relative prosperity, thanks largely to the sales of his best-selling book. He died in 1688, having caught a chill as he rode from Reading to London where he planned to act as peacemaker between a father and son.

If there is any doubt as to the influence over his writing of Bunyan's prison experience, one need only look to his sequel to *The Pilgrim's Progress*, which he wrote while free. It was called *The Life and Death of Mr Badman*, and flopped horribly.

Two Liverpool teenagers are introduced after a church fête

It's not an overly bold statement to claim that some first encounters between Britons have been of rather more significance than others. There was the meeting in Manchester's Midland Hotel in May 1904 of Charles Rolls and Frederick Royce. Dr Samuel Johnson marched into 6 Russell Street, Covent Garden to find one James Boswell within, apparently sipping a cup of tea. Henry Morton Stanley's encounter with Dr Livingstone even fashioned its own catchphrase. However, there can have been few meetings that have had such an impact on modern British culture than that which occurred on Saturday 6 July 1957.

The historic event happened in Woolton, a middle-class suburb of Liverpool. John Lennon's band, The Quarrymen – or 'The Quarry Men Skiffle Group' as the posters for the Woolton Parish Church Garden Fête dubbed them – were performing three times that day. First they played in the procession that opened the fête, although 'played' may be something of an exaggeration in this case. The lorry on the back of which they were standing was being driven very slowly through the streets of Woolton behind the float of the Rose Queen and her attendants, but the band members still found it difficult to keep from falling over, while at the same time doing something meaningful with their instruments.

John's half-sister Julia Baird, in her book *Imagine This*, remembers running alongside the lorry with her younger sister trying to make their big brother laugh. 'John gave up battling with balance,' she recalls, 'and sat with his legs hanging over the edge, playing his guitar and singing.'

The Quarrymen were awarded bottom billing on the poster for the fête, beneath such enticements as the Liverpool Police Dogs Display, Fancy Dress Parade, Sideshows, Refreshments, and the Band of the Cheshire Yeomanry. The entrance fee to this extravaganza was a modest 6d for adults and 3d for children. Undaunted by the apparent slight, the Quarrymen gave their second performance of the day, on a stage in a field by St Peter's, the parish church where John had once been a choir boy.

The line-up that day was John on vocals and guitar, Eric Griffiths on guitar, Rod Davis on banjo, with a rhythm section of Len Garry on tea-chest bass, Pete Shotton on washboard, and Colin Hanton on drums. In an interview with *Record Collector*, Paul McCartney recalls 'coming into the fête and seeing all the sideshows. And also hearing all this great music wafting in from this little tannoy system. It was John and the band. I remember I was amazed and thought, "Oh great," because I was obviously into the music.'

It's often cited that the two met at the fête. However, to be strictly accurate, although Paul heard John perform there, he was only introduced to him later, as the band was setting up for a gig across the road at the church hall. The Quarrymen (billed last again on the poster, of course) were to share duties with the George Edwards' Band at the Grand Dance that was scheduled to take place at 8P.M., after the garden fête – admission two shillings.

The unsung hero who brought John and Paul together was Ivan Vaughan. He knew both boys because he occasionally played the tea-chest bass with John's band and was in the same class at the Liverpool Institute as Paul. The two boys' interest in rock 'n' roll and their obvious talent at performing it was Vaughan's reason for making the introduction, though in another sense it was not a meeting of equals: Lennon would be 17 in October while Paul had only just turned 15.

The two talked a little – John may or may not have had a beer or two (Paul recalled smelling something beery on his breath) – before Paul famously showed John how to tune his guitar conventionally. Up until that time Lennon had been using a banjo tuning, in G (his banjo-playing mother Julia had taught him how to play guitar and had only ever shown him the banjo tuning). Paul had heard John play and sing earlier in the day but of course John had not heard what Paul could do. Cue an impromptu performance by the 15-year-old of a Little Richard medley, Gene Vincent's 'Be-Bop-A-Lula' and Eddie Cochran's 'Twenty Flight Rock'. Swapping the guitar for a handy piano that was lurking backstage, he also gave John his version of Jerry Lee Lewis' 'Whole Lotta Shakin' Goin' On'.

The Quarrymen performed their third gig of the day at the Grand Dance and the story goes that afterwards the band went to the pub, with McCartney and Vaughan in tow, though Quarrymen Len Garry and Pete Shotton have since claimed that that never happened (and, for that matter, that John had not been drinking earlier either). We do know what Paul and John were wearing when they met, though. Paul was rather dapper in a pair of black drainpipes and a white jacket with silvery streaks on it. Black-and-white photographs taken of the Quarrymen that day show John in an open-necked checked shirt, sleeves rolled to the elbows, and dark trousers.

Lennon was impressed by McCartney's singing and musicianship but he agonised over whether he should invite him to join the Quarrymen, fearing that Paul, despite his comparative youth, might prove a rival to his leadership of the band. After talking it over with washboard-player Pete Shotton, it was agreed to ask Paul to come on board. A fortnight or so later Pete bumped into Paul in Woolton and formally invited him to become a Quarryman. Paul recognised that John was talented but was somewhat less in awe of the other members of the band, so took his time deliberating before saying yes. Lennon and McCartney were in partnership. Paul's friend George Harrison joined the band the following year. In 1960, after several line-up and name changes ('Los Paranoias' perhaps being the best, with 'Japage 3' a low point), they became The Beatles. Ringo Starr joined two years later.

The effect that The Beatles had on music and culture in the 1960s was immense, not just in Britain but around the world. Although they split up somewhat acrimoniously in 1970, their output has remained incredibly popular, resulting in album sales of well over two billion. Their sound and style of songwriting has influenced musicians from Elton John to Florence and the Machine.

The band was such a force of nature that it seems highly unlikely that either Lennon or McCartney would have had as much of an influence as individual musicians had they never met. Post-Beatles, McCartney has produced some material that is more than passable, such as the *Band on the Run* album he made with Wings, and the occasional decent single. However, he has also seen fit to inflict on the world 'The Frog Chorus' and the interminable festive-season dirge 'Wonderful Christmastime'. Likewise, although there are plenty of fans of the solo work John produced before his life was tragically cut short in 1980, only a few tracks can make a serious claim to comparison with the best of The Beatles' canon.

Yoko Ono attempted to put her finger on the collaboration when commenting on an interview that she and John had given to *Rolling Stone* editor Jann Wenner in 1970:

> Paul possessed elements that John would have wanted to have as well. In other words, Paul was extremely charming to the world and, because of his diplomacy and charm I think that the band flourished in a way. Whereas John's rôle was to really bring that spiritually nourishing energy to the band, and that really helped the band to survive and to expand and to be successful... They were complementing each other.

There would not be another meeting that had an impact on British pop music that was in any way comparable for another 25 years, when an 18-year-old Johnny Marr turned up on the doorstep of Mrs Morrissey to see if her son was in.

The Duchess of Newcastle writes two remarkable addenda

The name of one of the most exceptional Britons of the 17th century is almost unknown nowadays. Margaret Cavendish, Duchess of Newcastle-upon-Tyne, chalked up many accomplishments in her 50-year life that would have been noteworthy even had she been born two centuries later. She was a scientist, philosopher, novelist, poet and playwright, sometimes combining two or more of these rôles in a single work. That she was able to achieve so much, despite the huge disadvantages she encountered in society on account of her sex, is testament to her brilliance and her unwillingness to accept that anything was impossible just because it had not been done before. This is certainly true of her autobiography – the first major secular memoir ever written by a woman. The fact that she also penned one of the very first works of a whole new genre of literature as something of an afterthought speaks volumes about the originality of her mind.

Cavendish was born Margaret Lucas in 1623, near Colchester in Essex, a child of two very wealthy parents. She was also a sister to a pair of fervent royalist brothers, a fact which, in those troubled times, was not necessarily a ticket to an easy life. After a childhood in which she was mainly self-taught (the presence of her tutors being 'rather for formality than benefit', as she put it), she became a maid of honour to Queen Henrietta Maria, the wife of Charles I, accompanying her fleeing mistress into exile in France in 1644. There she met and married the much older William Cavendish, then Marquess of Newcastle.

The couple moved to Antwerp, where the new marchioness was introduced to thinkers such as Thomas Hobbes and René Descartes. She began taking lessons in natural philosophy (what, nowadays, we would call science), a subject for which she had an exceptional flair. By 1652, she had moved beyond mere Hobbesian or Cartesian worlds and had begun to collate her own thoughts on the subject in a series of books. Four years later she published a prose and verse collection called *Nature's Pictures Drawn by Fancie's Pencil to the Life*. It spawned the first of her two extraordinary addenda. This was titled *A True Relation of my Birth, Breeding, and Life* – the first non-religious autobiography penned by a woman in the secular realm.

She returned to England with her husband in 1660 at the restoration of the monarchy and continued to write prolifically (she would go on to have 23 books published, including plays and collections of poetry). Although she was an individual given to eccentricities and consequently the butt of many a joke, she became recognised as England's first female scientist.

In 1666, by which time she had become a duchess, Cavendish published what would become the most well known of her half-dozen works on science, *Observations upon Experimental Philosophy*. This was a broadside aimed at what she saw as the rather fusty and closed-minded natural philosophers of her day. Cavendish railed at the reliance on theories about the motion of atoms to explain the world, believing herself that all atoms were 'animated with life and knowledge'. However, she was also one of the first natural philosophers to support Thomas Hobbes' argument that theology had no place in the world of scientific endeavour. It is her casual addendum to *Observations* that cemented her legacy in the world of literature as well as science, even if she receives little recognition in either field today.

The work she presented as an appendix she titled *The Blazing-World*. It is arguably the precursor to the whole genre of science fiction. It is also one of the first British novels ever written – it was published 12 years before John Bunyan's *The Pilgrim's Progress*, 22 years before Aphra Behn's masterpiece *Oroonoko*, and a full 53 years before Daniel Defoe's *Robinson Crusoe*.

It is appropriate that a book with such a title should come out in the year of the Great Fire of London, but its story has nothing to do with that holocaust and has a far wider reach than the mere destruction of a city. In her brief foreword 'To all Noble and Worthy Ladies', Cavendish declares that, 'The First Part is Romancical; the Second, Philosophical; and the Third is meerly Fancy; or (as I may call it) Fantastical.' She goes on to tell the following story.

A young woman is forced aboard a boat by a merchant who has fallen in love with her. A terrible storm sends the vessel up towards the North Pole and everyone on board freezes to death, except for the heroine. The boat sails onwards to a place where there is another pole close to the North Pole. This proves to be a portal to a separate planet: the eponymous Blazing-World, so called because it is lit by many Blazing-Starrs (*sic*). The world is populated by anthropomorphic beings such as bear-men, ape-men, fly-men, lice-men, spider-man and jackdaw-men, among numerous others. Each class of being has a specific task: for example, the fish-men are natural philosophers; giants are architects; bird-men are astronomers; and ape-men are chemists. Collectively, they decide to offer the new arrival as a wife to their emperor. He, taking her for some sort of goddess, proposes to worship her, an offer she declines. They marry, and the emperor 'gave her an absolute power to rule and govern all that World as she pleased. But her subjects, who could hardly be perswaded to believe her mortal, tender'd her all the Veneration and Worship due to a Deity.'

The new empress of Blazing-World embarks on a series of scientific and philosophical debates with the various species, who show off their respective knowledge and skills (the ape-men, for instance, unveil a method, including an egg-and-milk-only diet, that can give even an 'old decayed man' the body of a 20-year-old – neatly prefiguring the sort of quack remedies that make up the content of so much spam today). Many of these encounters end with the author demonstrating that nature is superior to the scientific instruments created by humans. That is not to say that the empress is in any way a Luddite, for she engages in speculations on natural philosophy and encourages scientific research.

It is at this point that Cavendish herself enters the fray as a soul or a spirit summoned up from the empress's home planet. Just in case the reader should be under any illusion about the identity of this spirit, she names her as the Duchess of Newcastle, someone who 'is not one of the most learned, eloquent, witty and ingenious, yet she is a plain and rational Writer'. The empress chooses her as her personal scribe and the two form a close platonic bond. This relationship is complicated somewhat when the empress forms a deep intellectual bond with the Duke of Newcastle. The duchess, briefly jealous, gets over it (thus assuring readers that they are engaging with a work of fiction).

The scene then moves to Welbeck Abbey, the duke and duchess's home in Sherwood Forest. A trial is held in the ducal seat in which the abstract notion of Fortune is set against Honesty and Prudence. Towards the end, Fortune storms off before Truth can deliver a verdict.

Trouble brews, for back in the world from which she had come, war breaks out. Most of the world's nations have formed an alliance and are attacking Esfi, the kingdom where the empress was born. She forms a navy/air force composed of fish-men, who can tow submarines using golden chains, and bird-men, who can fly up from the submarines to bomb the enemy with fire stones. Thus armed she returns to her own planet through a portal to fight against Esfi's enemies. As a result of her intervention, the king of Esfi is crowned ruler of the planet. The empress, her work done, returns to the Blazing-World to live a life of order and peace. The novel ends with the spirit of the duchess returning to her body back in Nottinghamshire where she regales her husband the duke with tales of the empress and her world.

It's quite clear that in *The Blazing-World*, Margaret Cavendish is imagining a world as she would like it, a world in which she is in control. Of course, such a state of affairs was simply not possible in the patriarchal society in which the author found herself, even though she had a certain amount of status by virtue of being a duchess. 'By this Poetical Description,' she told her readers, '...my ambition is not onely (*sic*) to be Empress, but Authoress of a whole World.' If she lacked power in the real world, she could at least take full control over the one she had imagined, 'That though I cannot be Henry the Fifth, or Charles the Second; yet, I will endeavour to be, Margaret the First.'

Her work might therefore also be considered the first feminist novel (albeit it's a man who eventually gets to rule the whole of the empress's home planet), beating Anne Brontë's *The Tenant of Wildfell Hall* to the punch by nearly two centuries.

The two addenda Cavendish wrote – *True Relation* and *The Blazing-World* – helped open up whole new vistas in literature. In the first, she established the notion that a woman might write her life story, even if she didn't find herself on the path to sainthood. In the second, she introduced many of the themes that form the bedrock of science fiction today, including the concept of portals into other worlds.

Never before or since have two literary B-sides made such an impact on the written word.

Four young Germans make a two-minute appearance on a television show about cutting-edge technology

'Television is called a medium,' so the quip goes, 'because it is neither rare nor well done.'

It's a joke often wrongly attributed to the late Patrick McGoohan, an actor now best remembered for his starring rôle as 'Number 6' in *The Prisoner*, a television series he devised himself and which quickly became a cult classic. His meditation on the nature of freedom and the limits of free will aired in the late 1960s and remains highly influential. It was an exceptional programme that perhaps proves the witticism's rule.

The Prisoner ran for 17 episodes, totalling over 13 hours of airtime. However, in 1975 it was a much shorter piece of footage – just 147 seconds – that was to show how television, for all its faults, could have a major impact on culture. In this case, it was the British music scene that was to be shaken up. The clip of four soberly dressed men from Düsseldorf wasn't broadcast on a music-based show, as one might expect, but on *Tomorrow's World*, the sensible-jumper-wearing, future-watching BBC series that ran from 1965 to 2003.

The four musicians were band co-founders Ralf Hütter and Florian Schneider, alongside Wolfgang Flür and Karl Bartos. Collectively they were Kraftwerk ('Power Station' in English) and very few of the British television-viewing public that night had heard their like before. The band are shown performing the first couple of minutes of 'Autobahn', their 22-minute homage to German motorways. The song starts with a cassette being loaded into a tape machine, which plays the sound of a car starting up and moving off. Half the band stands stiffly, picking at synthesisers, while the other half are seen 'apparently playing camping stoves with wired-up knitting needles' as journalist Andrew Harrison was to put it. The words to the song are all but whispered in a monotone between simple recurring synthesiser riffs. The whole is served up over complex repeated treble-heavy drumming patterns.

The meaning of the song would doubtless have been lost on most viewers, since the lyrics were in German:

'Wir fahr'n fahr'n fahr'n auf der Autobahn
Die Fahrbahn ist ein graues Band
Weisse Streifen, grüner Rand'

['We're driving driving driving on the Autobahn
The roadway is a grey track
White stripes, green edge']

After a minute of this, Raymond Baxter's reassuring matter-of-fact narration comes in to explain to viewers what it is that they're witnessing:

Kraftwerk have a name for this: it's Machine Music. The sounds are created at their laboratory in Düsseldorf, programmed, then recreated on stage with the minimum of fuss. This is 'Autobahn' – based, say the group, on the rhythm of trucks, cars and passing bridges heard while driving through Germany. Last year they removed the last recognisable instrument, a violin, and built these synthetic drums. Each disc gives a different sound – rolls, bongos, snares – just by completing the contact with the spring-steel batons. Next year Kraftwerk hope to eliminate the keyboards altogether and build jackets with electronic lapels which could be played by touch.

To put the song into context, this was the year when number ones in the British charts included 'If' by Telly Savalas, 'Bye Bye Baby' by the Bay City Rollers, and 'Whispering Grass' by television stars Windsor Davies and Don Estell (though, to be fair, 1975 did also throw up David Bowie's 'Space Oddity' and Queen's 'Bohemian Rhapsody').

The revolution did not occur overnight. The short clip did not cause every musician in Britain to swap their guitars and drums for synthesisers and electronic percussion, or eschew sentimental romantic ballads in favour of minimalistic lyricism about the stark realities of the industrial world – the following year saw Showaddywaddy, Brotherhood of Man and The Wurzels all topping the charts. However, the footage suddenly brought the band to the attention of a huge new audience and showed them that another way was possible. The *Guardian* newspaper, in its enduring wisdom, has since given its verdict on the *Tomorrow's World* appearance, calling it 'the germinating moment for British dance music'.

The first stirrings of change could be detected in Britain with the emergence of synthpop artists in the late '70s and early '80s, including The Human League, Gary Numan, Ultravox, Depeche Mode, Orchestral Manoeuvres in the Dark and Soft Cell. Other genres of music followed, all of which owed their roots to Kraftwerk: hip-hop, house, electro, drum and bass, techno, and more or less any other style that involved a synthesiser in some way. Musicians from David Bowie to Joy Division and Franz Ferdinand to Daft Punk have acknowledged Kraftwerk's influence on their output. As Martin Gore of Depeche Mode was keen to point out in an interview with journalist Neil McCormick, 'For anyone of our generation involved in electronic music, Kraftwerk were the godfathers... *Radio-Activity* in 1975, *Trans-Europe Express* in 1977, *The Man-Machine* in 1978: they still sound modern today. The electronic scene blew up after those pivotal albums.'

A three-minute version of 'Autobahn' reached number 11 in the charts in 1975 following the band's *Tomorrow's World* appearance. In 1981, Kraftwerk had a number-one hit in the UK with 'The Model'. This single went gold, selling over 500,000 copies. It had taken six years from their blink-and-you'll-miss-it appearance on British television for their sound to move from the extreme margins of popular taste to the mainstream. The band made a return to *Tomorrow's World* in 1991, only on that occasion they were represented by four robots (moving in sync to their chart hit, 'The Robots'). It was the logical extension of Kraftwerk's 'machine music' ethos.

Of the four members who made the historic appearance on *Tomorrow's World* back in 1975, only Ralf Hütter remains in the line-up today. As for the 'jackets with electronic lapels which could be played by touch', that's a technological leap that still remains to be taken.

A publisher cannot find anything interesting to read for his train journey home

Whisper it, but there was a time, before the internet and the smart phone and 4G networks, when it was possible to find oneself on a train and not have anything with which to amuse oneself besides the ever-changing scenery beyond the carriage window. For some people, staring out at the landscape and thinking deep thoughts is pleasure enough. However, for Allen Lane, in his early thirties but already a managing director of a publishing company, the want of a book to read caused him no end of irritation. And when one day he happened to be at Exeter St David's station with nothing to read and the prospect of a long journey back to London ahead of him, this event would change the face of publishing forever.

The incident is related on a page towards the back of a selection of Penguin paperbacks. Under the headline, 'He just wanted a book to read...' the tale is told in a single paragraph:

> 'Not too much to ask, is it?' It was in 1935 when Allen Lane, managing director of Bodley Head Publishers, stood on a platform at Exeter railway station looking for something good to read on his journey back to London. His choice was limited to popular magazines and poor-quality paperbacks – the same choice faced every day by the majority of readers, few of whom could afford hardbacks. Lane's disappointment and subsequent anger at the range of books generally available led him to found a company – and change the world.

Oddly, the date is wrong – Lane actually had his epiphany in 1934. The first Penguin paperbacks were launched in July 1935, which perhaps accounts for the error. He had just spent the weekend with the crime-fiction writer Agatha Christie, his favourite among the Bodley Head authors. On the train back to London he set his mind to devising a way of publishing good-quality titles in paperback for a mass market – the sort of books that could, perhaps, be sold on railway stations to bored travellers.

At the time, paperbacks were seen as trashy and, indeed, tended to live down to that reputation. The books that were published in paperback were overwhelmingly of the pulp-fiction variety, wrapped in lurid or crudely sexist covers. Only by buying a hardback book did the reader have any hope of encountering something of merit, and most people could not afford to indulge in such a luxury all that often. Lane's revolutionary idea was to make such books available for the knockdown price of 6d – the price of a packet of ten cigarettes. Having just spent the week in her company, no doubt Lane could already foresee paperback versions of Christie's books on sale up and down the country. He envisaged them being sold not just in shops but from vending machines as well (a dream that became reality when the first 'Penguincubator' was installed on the Charing Cross Road).

It is fair to say that his proposal did not go down at all well with his fellow directors at Bodley Head, who shared the commonly held view regarding the general undesirability of paperbacks and did not want to sully their company's products by offering them in that form. Only very reluctantly did they give Lane permission to try out his new venture, and even then they insisted that none of the work on it be done on company time.

It is possible that there was also some residual resentment towards Lane, since he was a cousin of the founder of Bodley Head, John Lane, and had been groomed from the age of 16 to rise through the ranks of the publishing company. On John Lane's death in 1925, Allen Lane became a director, and went on to chair the company five years later, a 20-something surrounded by men very much his senior in age and a great deal more conservative in their ways of doing business.

Thankfully, Lane could rely on help from his brothers, Dick and John. The three of them chose a name for their new imprint (Dolphin Books and Porpoise Books having been suggested and rejected), and despatched the young artist Edward Young to London Zoo to draw a penguin. The resultant sketch would become famous as the Penguin Books' colophon (though it would go through several tweaks over the years).

The covers Young proposed for the new company's books represented a sea change in paperback design. There would be no tacky illustrations – indeed, no illustrations at all – with the titles printed in clear black lettering across a band of white. To ease identification, each book would be coloured according to genre. Novels would be orange; dark blue was chosen for biographies; while crime-fiction titles would be green. As time went by, further genres were added and allotted their own colour: travel and adventure (cerise), drama (red), world affairs (grey), essays (purple), and miscellaneous (yellow). Only in later decades did Penguin paperbacks begin to be adorned (or defaced, according to your taste) with illustrations, but these were still a far cry from the tawdry drawings of the pulp-fiction merchants.

The imprint was launched on 30 July 1935, with an initial roster of ten paperbacks, including *A Farewell to Arms* by Ernest Hemingway and, of course, something by Agatha Christie: her first book, *The Mysterious Affair at Styles*. This had been published in hardback in the UK in 1921 and had actually made it into paperback form previously (in 1935) but at the higher price of 9d.

Each book in the series was allotted a number. This proved to be an astute move because it encouraged readers to start collecting them so that they might have the pleasure of owning the first ten or the first hundred and so on, even if some of the books might not particularly interest them. *Ariel*, a biography of Percy Bysshe Shelley by André Maurois, pipped Hemingway's novel of love and war to the honour of being number one.

Allen Lane declared later, 'We believed in the existence in this country of a vast reading public for intelligent books at a low price, and staked everything on it.' His bet came off in spades. Legend has it though that he did have one dicey moment before the launch had even occurred. It is said that the brilliantly titled fancy goods buyer at Woolworth's, an American named Clifford Prescott, was not enthusiastic about stocking the new imprint. When Lane gave his 15-minute pitch at Woolworth's executive office in Mayfair, Prescott was less than keen, telling the publisher that his books were not 'fancy' enough to be stocked. Customers, he claimed, liked their books to have hard covers adorned with colourful illustrations. It was vitally important for the Lane brothers to get into places like Woolworth's if they wanted to sell their books in high volumes, and this must have been a terrible blow to Allen. Thankfully, just as the audience with Prescott was ending, the American's wife happened to pop her head around the door. She had been on a rare shopping expedition in town and her husband had promised to take her out for lunch. Seeing the books on the table between the two men, she raved about how successful they were likely to be, saying that she herself would be likely to buy several every week. Prescott relented and ordered 36,000 copies. That figure soon rose to 63,000 as many of Lane's first ten titles sold out very swiftly. The Penguin imprint broke away from Bodley Head and on 1 January 1936 became a separate publishing company.

Soon Penguin was expanding into other areas of literature. Pelican Books was launched in 1937 to publish educational titles; Puffin Books began catering for children from 1940; the short-lived Ptarmigan was set up to appeal to the young adult market in 1945; and Penguin Classics started to reprint great works of literature from 1946.

The company's moment of greatest notoriety and, to many eyes, its finest hour, came in 1960, when Lane published an unexpurgated version of D.H. Lawrence's novel *Lady Chatterley's Lover* with the specific intention of challenging the Obscene Publications Act, which had come into force the year before. A trial ensued, which Lane won. The case was seen as a landmark victory for freedom of expression. It also gave to posterity the infamous observation made by lead prosecutor for the Crown, Mervyn Griffith-Jones, that Lawrence's novel was not a book that any upright citizen would wish his maidservant to read. Rarely can those in the upper reaches of the legal system have seemed more out of touch with ordinary citizens.

After Penguin, the culture of bookselling and book-reading in Britain changed completely. No longer was ownership of quality books the preserve of those well enough off to afford them. In the opening decades of the 20th century, it is true that those who could not afford to buy a book did have the opportunity to borrow them from a library, but not always for free. This was because many libraries were privately owned affairs run by such as Boots the Chemist (somewhat incongruously) and shops including W. H. Smith and Harrods, and there was a charge per book. The Public Libraries Act of 1850 had introduced the concept of the free council-run library, but Conservative MPs had opposed the bill so virulently in Parliament – fearing the consequences of an educated public – that the bill's guiding hand, Liberal politician William Ewart, was forced to make a raft of compromises that had severely limited the number of public libraries that were opened.

As Lane said himself in an interview with *The Bookseller* in May 1935, his imprint could be counted a triumph 'if these Penguins are the means of converting book-borrowers into book-buyers'. That they certainly did, as they proceeded to sell in their millions, spawning copycat imprints by other publishers.

Allen Lane was knighted for his services to publishing in 1952 and died of bowel cancer in 1970. Although he evidently revolutionised the way books were bought and sold in Britain, it's a sad fact that, were he to return to Exeter St David's station today, he would find the situation there much as he had encountered it back in 1934. As Caroline Lodge notes in her Book Word blog, 'At Exeter St David's station the only books sold today have to be tracked down in the dingy cave that is WH Smith's...The shop stocks bestsellers, fiction and nonfiction. Nothing I was tempted to buy and I doubt whether Allen Lane would have thought much of the selection either.' You can lead a railway station to literature, it would appear, but you may not be able to make it drink at the fount of knowledge for all that long.

Health & Safety

Derided as the product of the so-called
nanny state by people who would
clearly rather be ill and endangered,
the practice of 'health and safety' has
entered many areas of our national
life only after a tragic accident has
occurred. History is also littered with
inconsequential events in which a
reckless disregard for these two pillars
of prudence has had a disproportionate
effect on British life, for good or ill.

The people of Bradford briefly develop a taste for arsenic

'Bah! Humbug!' was famously a favourite expression of Ebenezer Scrooge, the miser who stomped grumpily about the novel *A Christmas Carol*. Back in 1843, when Charles Dickens was creating one of his most celebrated characters, he could not have known just how appropriate it would be to have put the word 'humbug' into such a poisonous character's mouth.

Just 15 years later, a simple misunderstanding brought about one of the worst cases of mass poisoning in Britain and it was all caused by a single batch of humbugs.

Arsenic was the poison involved. It occurs naturally in a large range of minerals, and although nowadays the substance tends to be associated with the likes of Agatha Christie and Dorothy L. Sayers, its toxic properties have been known since time immemorial. Many is the tale of an ancient Greek or Roman being done away with by an unscrupulous rival with a grudge and access to a pinch of arsenic.

Sugary sweets, of course, are far more recent victuals. In Victorian times, sugar beet had yet to make its arrival on the flat fields of the Fens, and Britain had to import every last teaspoonful of the sugar it ate, as it had always done. When the new and exciting foodstuff first came to Britain, probably in the mid-13th century, it was so expensive that it was the preserve of royalty alone. It was the capture, transportation and enslavement of Africans in the 17th century that really began to bring the price of sugar down. Large plantations, worked by slaves, were established in the West Indies, with the cane sent to Britain to be refined.

Huge fortunes could be made from the sale of 'white gold'. Keenly aware of this, successive governments set high taxes on the commodity. So it was that, come 1858, the price of sugar made it a treat for a special occasion rather than the staple it has become in modern times. It would not be until 1874 and the abolition of the sugar tax that molasses became affordable to the masses.

Much in the same way that Class A drugs today are often cut with talcum powder or some other such matter in order to maximise profits, in the 19th century, unprincipled sugar dealers would covertly bulk up their merchandise by adding something that looked like sugar but was much cheaper. A common additive – known as 'daft' – typically consisted of powdered limestone and/or gypsum (as used in plaster casts). The resulting product could then be sold at a price more within the budget of the working classes, thus opening a huge market to the sugar merchants.

In October 1858, William Hardaker was working at his confectionery stall at the Green Market in Bradford. Well known in the area, he had been nicknamed 'Humbug Billy' by the locals. His humbugs were styled 'lozenges' because they were believed to have some mild medicinal effect on account of the peppermint they contained. He did not make the boiled sweets himself but procured them from a spice dealer called Joseph Neal. He in turn sourced his daft (gypsum in this case) from a pharmacist named Charles Hodgson in Shipley, three miles away. On 18 October, Neal sent out an employee, John Archer, to pick up some gypsum from Hodgson.

In the days following the poisoning, the police pieced together what had happened next. Archer had evidently travelled to the pharmacy as he was told. Hodgson was on the premises but was feeling unwell, so his assistant, William Goddard, had attended to the customer. Unsure of the location of the gypsum, the young Goddard had sought out Hodgson, who had informed him that he would find it in a cask in a certain corner of the attic. Goddard had served Archer and the latter had returned to his employer with

12lb of white powder. This was handed to a man called James Appleton, who was to make up a batch of humbugs. He used 40lb of sugar, 12lb of daft, 4lb of gum and some peppermint oil and soon had a large quantity of confectionery ready for distribution. The sweets had turned out a slightly different colour than usual but not so dramatically as to drive Appleton to any great speculation as to why. The confectioner, who appears not to have been a very inquiring soul, was poorly for a few days afterwards but had put it down to a cold and had thought no more about it. Hardaker came by on the Saturday to buy some humbugs for his stall. He, too, queried the humbugs' change of hue but Neal put it down to a new batch of gum that Appleton had used. To mollify Hardaker, the spice dealer knocked a ha'penny per pound off the price.

That same weekend, a Bradford man named Mark Burran had stopped by at Humbug Bill's stall to purchase some of the sweets. He went home and gave one each to his two sons, five-year-old Orlando and John, a toddler. It wasn't long before he was obliged to call John Bell, a local doctor, to the family home. Both boys had become extremely ill and, despite the physician's efforts, they died on the Sunday evening. Although it was suggested that the cause might have been cholera, the doctor suspected that they had been poisoned and the police were called in.

Before long, the local constabulary was overwhelmed with accounts of mysterious illnesses and deaths occurring all over Bradford. It didn't take the deductive power of a Sherlock Holmes to work out that the one element tying the victims together was that they had all eaten humbugs bought at Hardaker's stall in the Green Market. Officers learnt the sweet-seller's address and called round. They were surprised to find that he, too, was unwell.

Having questioned Hardaker as to his supplier – and taken some of his humbugs for analysis – they spoke next to Joseph Neal. The spice dealer was the first person to point the finger of suspicion at the daft that had been used in the mix. Moving on to Charles

Hodgson's pharmacy in Shipley, the police quite naturally followed up on this hypothesis. One can only imagine the horror-stricken look on the pharmacist's face when it became apparent that Goddard had misunderstood his instructions and had taken the powder not from a cask that contained gypsum but from one that held arsenic trioxide. Aside from sharing a colour, the two powders are both odourless and tasteless, making the error only too easy to commit.

The good citizens of Bradford buried their dead. In all, 20 people – mostly children – had perished from eating the corrupted humbugs while around 200 others suffered the lesser but still very unpleasant effects of arsenical poisoning – stomach cramps, convulsions, vomiting of bile and blood, diarrhoea, delirium and shock. Despite this, the survivors could count themselves very lucky indeed, because it was estimated that a single humbug contained over one-and-a-half times the dose necessary to finish a person off in ordinary circumstances.

Three arrests were made. First, William Goddard was seized and brought before the local magistrates on 1 November 1858. Pharmacist Charles Hodgson and spice-dealer Joseph Neal were then charged with manslaughter alongside the hapless assistant. Charges against Goddard and Neal were subsequently dropped and Hodgson was acquitted at York Assizes in December.

Dickens had *A Christmas Carol* end happily, with Scrooge seeing the error of his ways and finding redemption. Likewise, there is a silver lining to the sorry tale of the Bradford humbug poisonings. The hullaballoo that ensued contributed in no small measure to the passing in 1860 of The Adulteration of Food and Drink Act, which regulated what could be added to foodstuffs. This was followed in 1868 by The Pharmacy Act, which tightened up the procedures that pharmacists had to follow regarding poisons. This included a requirement for the purchaser of a poison to sign for it in a pharmacist's register – a stipulation beloved of crime writers of a certain era.

These laws are the forerunners of modern-day legislation designed to shield us from adulterated food and drink. Progress on this front is not a given, however, for such protections may well find themselves watered down by transatlantic trade deals and Britain's planned departure of the European Union, an organisation that has very strict food regulations in place. In the meantime, with Britain beset by an obesity crisis, the government has announced the introduction of the first sugar tax in nearly 150 years, albeit one that applies only to soft drinks. It's ironic, given the tragedy that occurred in Bradford when all eyes were on the arsenical content of the humbugs, that sugar is now recognised as something of a poison itself.

Henry I indulges in a few lampreys too many

It's a curious thing that two words – 'surfeit' and 'lampreys' – are seldom uttered in English nowadays unless they are used together in an infamous phrase to describe the cause of death of Henry I. Of all the myriad ways it was possible to meet one's end in the Norman era, it took a king to bring about his own demise by consuming 'a surfeit of lampreys'. We can only speculate as to how many further violent deaths might have been avoided in the 18-year civil war that followed his untimely death had William the Conqueror's fourth son had the willpower to temper his ichthyophagous gluttony. On a more positive note, Henry's rash decision to fill his belly with this barely edible eel-like fish would eventually lead to the drawing up of arguably the most important document in the history of the nation.

Henry was born two (or possibly three) years after his father's 1066 invasion of England. He seized the throne in 1100, when the king, William Rufus (one of his older brothers), was killed by an arrow in a hunting accident in the New Forest. No sooner installed he married Matilda, daughter of King Malcolm III of Scotland, and defeated the forces of his older brother, Robert, thus securing the throne.

So began Henry's 35-year reign over England and Normandy. It was characterised by the monarch's efficiency, a virtue only soured by his tendency to ruthlessness. All would perhaps have been well, had his only legitimate son and heir, William Adelin, not been drowned along with 300 others when a vessel called *White Ship* went down in the English Channel in 1120.

Matilda of Scotland had died two years earlier, so Henry swiftly married one Adeliza of Louvain in the hope of producing a new heir. Unfortunately, this union proved fruitless, and so Henry was forced to choose a successor from a group that included his daughter Matilda, his illegitimate son Robert (the Earl of Gloucester) and his nephews. The most likely of this last set to gain the avuncular blessing was Stephen of Blois (who was married to yet another Matilda).

In 1127, Henry declared that, on his death, his daughter would become queen. It was unusual to choose a female successor but there were no hard-and-fast rules laid down regarding succession to the throne and Matilda was the pragmatic choice. In preparation, Henry married her off to Geoffrey of Anjou, hoping to rebuild an alliance with that state. This proved a not altogether happy choice, since the couple turned not only against each other but, when they became reconciled, then turned against the king. They were incensed when he refused their requests to cede castles in Normandy to Matilda or to compel his Norman nobles to swear an oath of loyalty to her – moves that would have strengthened her claim to the crown. Normandy and Anjou shared a frontier and, as relations between Henry and his daughter and son-in-law deteriorated, the king spent his final months hurriedly reinforcing the border against his southern neighbour.

It is at this troubled time, towards the end of November 1135, that a desire to go hunting brought Henry to the forest of Lyons in Normandy. The king was in his mid-sixties – a grand old age in those days – and had habitually enjoyed unusually robust health. There is no reason to suspect that this was not the case when he arrived at the forest. What happened next was set down by the chronicler Roger of Wendover:

> Henry... stopped at St. Denys in the wood of Lions [sic] to eat some lampreys, a fish he was very fond of, though they always disagreed with him, and the physicians had often cautioned him against eating them, but he would not listen

to their advice. This food mortally chilled the old man's blood and caused a sudden and violent illness against which nature struggled and brought on an acute fever in an effort to resist the worst effects of the disease.

The lamprey is not one of Nature's most delightful creatures. It is a fish that resembles an eel and some species are parasitic, feeding on their prey by attaching their jawless sucker mouths onto them. The historical novelist Elizabeth Chadwick has offered a compelling theory as to why Henry's physicians might have been so opposed to the king consuming this particular fish. The medieval outlook on nutrition, she points out, was to categorise all foods in one of four humours: Sanguine (warm and moist), Phlegm (cold and moist), Melancholic (cold and dry) and Yellow Bile (warm and dry). The ideal diet included foods from all four humours, which would provide the body with a healthy balance. However, those who were advanced in years were advised to err on the side of the warm humours – particularly the dry Yellow Bile. Lampreys, by contrast, were almost off the scale in terms of their perceived coldness and wetness, putting them at the extreme end of the Phlegm humour.

Hence it must have come as no great surprise to his physicians when Henry became seriously ill (it's quite possible that the lampreys – fish that can prove toxic at the best of times – simply gave him severe food poisoning or brought on dysentery). After hanging on valiantly for up to a week, the king died on 1 December 1135. His corpse was taken to Rouen where it began to decompose rather unpleasantly. Roger of Wendover relates that, at length, a physician was paid a large sum of money to conduct the unpleasant task of extracting the king's brain with a hatchet in order to bury it separately, as was the custom. '...notwithstanding that the head was wrapped up in several napkins, [the physician] was poisoned by the noisesome smell, and thus the money which he received was fatal to him; he was the last of King Henry's victims, for he had killed many before.'

Henry had clearly not anticipated dying at this juncture. It may be expected that a man concerned for his legacy would have ensured a smooth transition of power after his death, and Henry no doubt imagined that he still had plenty of time to arrange matters to this end. He could either ensure that Matilda was in such a position of power and authority that her coronation would go unopposed; or jettison her altogether and give sufficient backing to one of the other prospective candidates to enable them to ascend to the throne unchallenged. As it was, at the time of his death, he was attempting to suppress a rebellion of nobles in southern Normandy who were supported by Matilda and Geoffrey. Thus, he was in the awkward position of being in a military conflict in which he was opposed by his daughter, the woman he had publicly chosen as his successor.

It's little wonder that things went haywire as soon as the lampreys had wreaked their revenge on Henry. As the late king's anointed heir, Matilda claimed the throne of England and Normandy for herself. The Norman nobles, for their part, favoured Henry's nephew, Theobald of Blois. However, it was his younger brother, Stephen of Blois, who was first off the mark, crossing the Channel from Boulogne to be crowned on 22 December 1135. The inevitable civil war that followed lasted until 1153 and threw the nation into such utter disarray that the period gained the name the Anarchy. Such was the dark horror of this time that *The Anglo-Saxon Chronicle* recorded that 'men said openly that Christ and his saints were asleep'.

Stephen, though a brave soldier, was not a slick political operator and quickly alienated the nobles and clergy whose support he needed to secure his throne. One particular enemy he made was Henry's illegitimate son, Robert, the 1st Earl of Gloucester. As a result, Robert joined forces with Matilda when she arrived in England in 1139. Bitter and bloody war commenced, ending in February 1141 with Stephen defeated and captured at the Battle of Lincoln.

Opposition to Matilda in London meant that she was never crowned. However, her condescension and arrogance showed her to be as unfitted to the rôle of queen of England as Stephen had been to be king. Playing on the would-be monarch's unpopularity, Stephen's wife – who until recently had actually been Queen Matilda herself – marshalled her own army and war broke out again. There is a faintly comic element to this new twist, for it left both sides declaring their allegiance to Matilda, then having to clarify which one they meant. Sadly, violence rather than hilarity ensued, leading to Robert of Gloucester falling prisoner at Winchester to the former Queen Matilda. The latter was able to exchange Robert for her captured husband in a prisoner swap, and Stephen promptly declared himself king again. He and his wife, Matilda, enjoyed their second coronation at Christmas 1141. The war continued with neither side gaining the upper hand until Robert died in October 1147. With her key ally gone, Henry's daughter retreated to Normandy the following year.

However, this did not bring an end to the bloodshed. The cudgels were taken up by Matilda's son, Henry, on his mother's behalf and the conflict dragged on. Eventually, the nobles became sick of the seemingly interminable warfare and took the expedient step of refusing to go on fighting one another. This sage, if overdue, resolution led to the end of the civil war in 1153, with Stephen and Henry being cajoled into signing the Treaty of Winchester. This agreement decreed that Stephen would remain on the throne until his death, when Henry would become king. Stephen died the following year and Henry II (see page 124) reigned for 35 years, just as his grandfather and namesake had done.

The Anarchy had been both a devastating and debilitating experience for the nation but it had one notable effect: it increased the power of the nobles to a point where they could force their own monarch into making peace. Just over six decades after the end of the war, the barons would flex this political muscle in boldly forcing King John to sign the Magna Carta.

And none of this might have come to pass had Henry simply leaned back in his chair after a lamprey or two and said, 'I think that's probably enough for now.'

A key to a locker is accidentally taken off a ship

The sorry tale of the *Titanic's* maiden voyage has become the best-known shipwreck story of modern times and an abject lesson in the dangers of hubris. Heading for New York from Southampton, the 46,000-tonne cruise liner struck an iceberg in the North Atlantic at 11.40P.M. on 14 April 1912. Although supposedly unsinkable, she slipped beneath the waves at 2.20A.M., just two hours and forty minutes later. Of the roughly 2,220 passengers and crew on board, only 705 survived.

Official inquiries in the UK and the US were held into what went wrong that night. An ocean of ink has been since expended pointing the finger of blame at the various actors in the tragedy. These included Thomas Andrews, a key member of the *Titanic's* design team, who had failed to make the bulkheads (the walls between the ship's compartments) high enough to prevent seawater from flooding the vessel. J. Bruce Ismay, managing director of the White Star Line, had cut costs by supplying only enough lifeboats for 1,178 people, and had exacerbated matters by not devising an evacuation plan, having assumed it would be not be necessary. Captain Edward Smith had ignored half a dozen reports of ice and had recklessly cruised through dangerous waters at night without reducing speed. Andrews went down with the ship. Smith either did likewise or was drowned soon afterwards. Ismay, controversially, took one of the places in the lifeboats and was saved.

However, if it were not for one small detail – a mistake over a key to a locker – none of the above might have occurred.

At the last minute, the White Star Line transferred Henry Tingle Wilde from the *Olympic* to the *Titanic*, her sister ship, on the grounds that his experience as an officer would come in useful on a maiden voyage on which there might be teething troubles. Wilde took the post of chief officer, which meant that the *Titanic*'s principal officers were all reduced in rank. The former chief officer became the first officer; the first officer became the second officer; and the second officer, David Blair, rather than becoming third officer, was removed from the ship's roster altogether.

Blair left the ship on being told he was surplus to requirements. Unfortunately, he forgot to leave the key for the crow's-nest locker that contained a pair of binoculars. Although these were not intended specifically for those on lookout duty to use, had they had the key they would certainly have had access to them. On the voyage, lookout George Symons went to the officers' mess to request a pair (there were five others on board for the use of various officers) but was told there were none spare.

Frederick Fleet, one of the lookouts on duty at the time of the collision, later found himself questioned at the inquiry organised by the US Congress. Asked whether he or fellow lookout Reginald Lee might have spotted the iceberg earlier had binoculars been available, he responded that he would have seen it 'a bit sooner'. When asked how much sooner, he replied, 'Well, enough to get out of the way.'

There were arguments put forward at the time (and since) that binoculars were neither a necessary nor even a desirable piece of equipment for those on lookout to possess. The reasoning is that there is a danger that those on duty might stop taking in the general view around them and instead concentrate on the much smaller area that can be seen at any one time through binoculars. They might also become fascinated by the inspection of something they have seen and thus delay their reporting of it (which was done by ringing a bell). However, another *Titanic* lookout, George Hogg, reported that he had used them while working on the

Adriatic, another White Star Line ship, and Fleet testified that there had been binoculars supplied during all four years of his duty on board the same company's *Oceanic*. Although binoculars were more often used to confirm a possible sighting of an object, a light or a ship once it had been picked up by the naked eye – and both Hogg and Symons testified that they would only use binoculars in this manner – Fleet claimed that he would have employed them 'constantly... to pick out things on the horizon' on the night the *Titanic* sank.

The scale of the disaster might still have been much reduced had it not been for another unfortunate occurrence. Between five and ten miles from the *Titanic*, a 6,000-tonne cargo vessel called the *Californian* had come to a halt. Unlike Captain Smith, the *Californian's* skipper, Stanley Lord, had taken heed of the ice warnings and had stopped his ship's engines to wait until the dawn brought a chance to see where he was going.

The wireless operator on duty on the *Californian* that night was the inexperienced Cyril Evans. To be fair to him, most wireless operators were inexperienced in 1912, since the technology was still a novelty and its performance frustratingly erratic. At some time just after 11P.M. on the fateful night he had sent an inappropriately jocular message to the *Titanic:* 'Say old man we are surrounded by ice and stopped'. Evans had been sharply berated by John Phillips, the on-duty wireless operator of the *Titanic*, who was busy sending other signals and who replied telling him to 'shut up'.

This rebuke may well have contributed to Evans' decision to close down his set at 11.30P.M. A little later, he was visited in his wireless shack by Third Officer Charles Groves, who was always keen to find out what news Evans had received from the outside world. He had even started dabbling with the basics of wireless telegraphy himself and had reached a reasonable proficiency. That night, while Evans read a magazine, Groves slipped the headphones on to have a listen. Unfortunately, according to Walter

Lord's classic account of the sinking, *A Night to Remember*, 'The *Californian's* set had a magnetic detector that ran by clockwork. Groves didn't wind it up, and so heard nothing.' He removed the headphones and wandered off. It was just after 12.15A.M.

Had Groves known enough about the *Californian's* wireless set to wind it up, he might well have heard the first distress calls broadcast by the *Titanic* at around 12.15A.M. That being the case, he might well have been able to persuade his captain to go to the *Titanic's* aid. Since the *Californian* was so close, it's very likely that all the passengers and crew could have been transferred from the sinking ship and no loss of life would have occurred. As it was, although there was plenty of other evidence that a ship near the *Californian* was in trouble, Lord was able to interpret it in ways that excused him from navigating his way cautiously through the icebergs to help. After the *Californian*, the closest ship to the scene was the *Carpathia*. She was 58 miles away when her captain, Arthur Rostron, learnt of the *Titanic's* plight from one of his wireless operators. Despite bravely putting on full steam through the ice-strewn waters, Rostron arrived one hour forty minutes after the sinking had taken place and was therefore only able to save those in the lifeboats.

The sinking of the *Titanic* is a tragedy to which many myths have attached themselves, limpet-like. The band went down playing *Nearer my God to Thee* (they didn't, though they might have played a hymn called *Autumn* until quite near the end); a man managed to save himself by dressing up as a woman (there is no evidence for this); the ship was carrying a cargo of gold and gems (it wasn't, though there were one or two valuable items lost, such as an oil painting by the French artist Merry-Joseph Blondel).

We are on much more solid ground when we consider the repercussions of the disaster. Indeed, the only redeeming feature of the sinking of the *Titanic* is that the death toll was so great that it simply could not be ignored. The most immediate and obvious consequence was that thenceforth ship captains took warnings of ice much more seriously and either slowed down when in a danger area or avoided it altogether. The International Ice Patrol was established – a cooperative venture by the US and UK authorities – and the 'winter lane' for shipping in the North Atlantic was moved further south.

The nonsensical formula laid down by the Board of Trade that stipulated the lifeboat provision on ships was scrapped. According to Walter Lord, the regulations stated that, 'All British vessels over 10,000 tonnes must carry 16 lifeboats with a capacity of 5,500 cubic feet, plus enough rafts and floats for 75 per cent of the capacity of the lifeboats.' When applied to the *Titanic*, it meant that she was required to carry lifeboats for just 962 people even though, at full capacity, she would have had over 3,300 passengers and crew on board. A new simple rule was established: there must always be enough room in the lifeboats for everyone. Furthermore, passengers travelling in first class would no longer receive preferential access to the lifeboats. Such a convention had resulted in 58 first-class male passengers being saved from the *Titanic* while 53 steerage-class minors had perished – so much for 'women and children first'.

Ship designers took note of the foolhardy behaviour of Harland and Wolff, the Belfast shipyard charged by the White Star Line to draw up the plans for the *Titanic*. Aside from their designers' failure to build the bulkheads high enough, they had assumed that only one would ever be breached in an accident, with the result that no more than two compartments would be flooded. The iceberg that did for the *Titanic* had smashed into her starboard side, creating huge openings in the hull below the waterline and allowing the sea to enter no fewer than five of the ship's compartments.

Two years after the accident, and as a direct result of it, the International Convention for the Safety of Life at Sea (SOLAS) was set in place. Over a century later, the protocol remains in force. Among other safety measures, these regulations obliged all ships to maintain a 24-hour radio watch. There would be no more calamities caused by a wireless set being shut down at night. The loss of the *Titanic* also brought home to stock-market investors the potential value of wireless telegraphy to the safety of shipping. In the immediate aftermath of the catastrophe, shares in Marconi went stratospheric. It would seem that there is seldom a wind so ill that it blows nobody any good...

An insect conspires against an emperor

Britain is a nation forged by a series of invasions from antiquity. The Romans, Franks, Scots (who, confusingly, came from Ireland), Angles, Saxons, Jutes, Norsefolk and Normans have all in their turn helped shaped the nation, doubtless drawn to it on account of its enchanting weather and sophisticated cuisine. Even the Celts and Picts – peoples generally thought of as indigenous to Britain – are believed only to have arrived in the Bronze Age. However, there is an argument to be made that the nation has been even more greatly influenced by an invasion in the distant past that did not take place.

In AD 540, things were looking up for Byzantine emperor Justinian I. The ruler of the Eastern Roman Empire seemed well on his way to realising his dream of reconquering the western half of the empire, which had been taken by Vandals, Ostrogoths, Visigoths and sundry other enemies. Justinian had made a somewhat precarious peace with Persia, allowing him to launch a military campaign westward from Byzantium (modern-day Istanbul). His troops, usually led by General Belisarius, had recaptured territories in northern Africa, including the prize city of Carthage. The islands of Sardinia and Corsica were reconquered, as were the Balearic Islands off Spain. Then came Sicily, Naples and the real jewel in the crown, Rome. By the time of his death in AD 565, Justinian the Great, as he became, had restored the vast majority of the Roman Empire's frontiers to their heyday, albeit he'd had to leave the trouncing of his foes in Gaul to his allies, the Franks.

There was just one glaring omission: Britain. Although never fully conquered by his predecessors, the island had been largely Roman for more than three centuries, providing the empire with its famous northern frontier at Hadrian's Wall (and briefly even further north along the Antonine Wall, stretched out across what is now Scotland's Central Belt). Yet it was the one major territory that remained beyond Justinian's grasp.

It should not have been so. In the middle of the 6th century, a cleric named Gildas wrote a tract called *De Excidio Britanniae (The Ruin of Britain)*, an excoriating attack on British society which, writing as a former hermit on the spartan island of Steep Holm, he felt had rather gone to the bad. He tells us that after the Battle of Mount Badon, in which the Britons under one Ambrosius Aurelianus (taken by some historians to be none other than King Arthur) scored a famous victory over the invading Angles and Saxons, no foreign attacks occurred for half a century or so. However, the country remained divided into several small competing kingdoms. Gildas also records that in AD 537 a good king (also supposed by some to be King Arthur, though the writer doesn't name him) was murdered by his evil nephew – a deed that throws southern Britain into a state of turmoil. With the various surviving British kings forever at each other's throats, the island was enfeebled and ripe for the 6th-century Romans to follow in the footsteps of emperors Julius Caesar and Claudius and land an army on a British shore.

Justinian clearly felt that this was the case. He was already using Britain as a bargaining chip in negotiations with the Ostrogoths in Italy, claiming that it was in his power to exchange it with them for Sicily. As it happened though, his designs were thwarted by a tiny insect from the order *Siphonaptera*. The bubonic plague – spread by the bite of fleas carried on the backs of rats – broke out in Egypt in 541. Merchant ships unwittingly ferried the flea-ridden rats around the Mediterranean and inevitably Byzantium was soon wracked by the disease.

The plague may well have been triggered by an extreme natural disaster that occurred in 536, which brought about what is known as the Late Antique Little Ice Age. This was caused by a blanket of dust in the atmosphere that covered the globe and blocked out a great deal of the Sun's heat. This, in turn, made the Earth cool dramatically, causing chaotic weather events such as snow in summer. It's not clear exactly what produced the dust cloud, though the most likely explanation is a catastrophic eruption from a volcano such as Krakatoa, Ilopango or the Rabaul caldera. The historian Procopius, who lived through the event, inevitably saw it as a bad omen. 'During this year [536], a most dread portent took place,' he recorded, 'for the sun gave forth its light without brightness.'

Although Byzantium was worst hit by the plague (Procopius noted with revulsion that the entire city stank of the dead), it became a true pandemic, wiping out tens of millions of people in countries around the world, including Britain and Ireland. It caused famine in Europe through the wholesale disruption of agriculture and eventually wiped out more than 10 per cent of the world's population. The disaster became known as the Plague of Justinian, and was a pestilence to which even emperors were not immune, for one day a flea dared to land on Justinian himself and bite into the patrician skin. The emperor came down with the plague. Though he recovered after a few months, his illness threw his plans into disarray and the reconquest of Britain by Rome was never a serious consideration again.

It's interesting to speculate what might have occurred had Justinian not been knocked off course by the plague and had succeeded in re-assimilating Britain into the Roman Empire. Although Scotland might well have proved unconquerable again, it's quite possible that an island once more stabilised by *Pax Romana* (up to Hadrian's Wall at least) would not have atomised into the seven English kingdoms (Wessex, Kent, Sussex, Essex, East Anglia, Mercia and Northumbria), Cornwall and Wales, as had actually happened by the following century. Had this more united nation been able to see off the many invasions that were to come over the next few hundred years, not only British history but the make-up of its people might be very different today.

A bacteriologist sneaks off on holiday without doing the washing-up

Carelessness and untidiness are not the sort of characteristics that most parents try to instil in their offspring. Rather they are apt to warn their children that these are the kind of traits that will inevitably lead to a life of dissipation or, at best, barely managed chaos. However, there are occasions when such habits can actually be advantageous. For example, the most famous happy accident in medical history occurred only because two exceedingly trivial details in a man's life coincided, neither of which would have happened had it not been for an act of carelessness combined with a little devil-may-care untidiness.

The man in question was Alexander Fleming. Born in 1881 on a farm in Ayrshire, Fleming studied medicine and became a bacteriologist at St Mary's Hospital in Paddington, West London. His research and lecturing were interrupted by World War I, during which he served as a captain in the Royal Army Medical Corps. Attending to wounded soldiers in hospitals just behind the lines in France, he witnessed many deaths due to infected wounds. Antiseptics – as pioneered by the surgeon Joseph Lister – were used extensively by British army doctors. However, Fleming noticed that while they were effective when used to treat superficial injuries, they killed more soldiers than they cured when applied to deeper wounds. After the war he returned to St Mary's with a renewed vigour, determined to find some way of defeating the bacteria that infected these more serious traumas.

He thought he had made a breakthrough in 1923, when his tests established that nasal mucus slowed down the growth of bacteria. The enzyme responsible, lysozyme, can also be found in saliva, tears, hair and skin as well as in egg whites. It was a previously unknown enzyme and its discovery put Fleming's name on the map. Unfortunately, it was not the remedy he had hoped for, because it proved effective only against bacteria that were harmless.

It was five years later, when Fleming was working on the influenza virus, that he took the huge step forward for which he had been striving so long. Ironically, it occurred because he went on a month's holiday (not a fortnight's break, as is often erroneously reported). Rather than washing up all his petri dishes (he had been growing the staphylococcus bacteria to use in his experiments) and tidying them away in a cupboard, he left them piled up in the sink. Furthermore, no doubt demob-happy at the thought of his break at his family's country house near Newmarket in Suffolk, he did not notice that a window to the street had been left open.

When he came back, on Friday 28 September 1928, he went to the sink to start on the task he should properly have carried out a month beforehand. He might well have cleaned everything up and started back on his work, but he noticed something curious in one of the petri dishes in which he had been growing the bacteria: a sort of blue-green mould had established itself. While Fleming had been sunning himself in Suffolk, it had been busily expanding across the glass, creating a halo that was entirely free of the staphylococcus bacteria. The mould, which had blown in through the window by chance, was *Penicillium notatum*.

This did not constitute the discovery of penicillin, as is often reported. Although it's true that Fleming did coin the word, the penicillium mould had been identified at least 40 years beforehand. Joseph Lister himself had experimented with it on humans with some success, although there's no evidence that Fleming knew about his fellow scientist's research. What's more, although Fleming published his own research the following year and also achieved some favourable outcomes when treating patients, he found the mould very difficult to cultivate in any quantity and his research into penicillin became somewhat fitful.

It did not help that he was not a great communicator and so had found it difficult to enthuse others with his work. By 1940 he had given up altogether. Thankfully, an Australian pharmacologist called Howard Florey at Oxford University had come across Fleming's research and decided to carry out his own investigations. He put together a team of scientists that included Ernst Chain – a German Jew who was expert in pathology and had fled Hitler's Reich – and Norman Heatley, who was greatly skilled in the micro-analysis of organic substances. Florey's team developed penicillin further, purifying it to such an extent that in 1940 they were able to cure infections in mice. Like Fleming, they also found it difficult to produce the drug in any quantity. Although they had come up with a method of mass-producing it in the laboratory, they still couldn't manage the sort of yields that would make its use practicable.

Successful trials followed in 1941 at Oxford's Radcliffe Infirmary, but these were still very small scale, so Florey and Heatley crossed the Atlantic to attempt to talk pharmaceutical companies into manufacturing the drug. Even though their offer was taken up, by the summer of 1942 there had only been enough penicillin created in the US to treat ten patients. It took a chemical engineer called Margaret Hutchinson Rousseau to break the logjam, developing a process of deep-tank fermentation using corn steep liquor. In 1943, the Northern Regional Research Laboratory at Peoria, Illinois, instigated a global search for the best mould to use in the fermentation process. As it happened, the ideal candidate proved to be close at hand – a rotting cantaloupe melon found in a Peoria market was found to contain an excellent mould for the job. By the time of the Normandy landings, 2.3 million doses of penicillin had been prepared. By the end of the war, this figure had risen to hundreds of billions of doses.

The introduction of penicillin by the Allies in the latter stages of World War II was very effective in combatting septicaemia and gangrene, both of which could turn a run-of-the-mill wound into a fatal one. The Axis forces did not have access to the drug and, as a consequence, the survival and recovery rates of the latter's injured troops was markedly lower. In this way, the open window and the dirty petri dish back in 1928 made their contribution to the war effort. Penicillin was also found to work extremely well against bacterial diseases such as typhoid and tuberculosis, which were rife at the time.

Given the massive and immediate impact penicillin had, it's unsurprising that Fleming, Florey and Chain did not have long to wait for their efforts to be recognised. The three were jointly awarded the Nobel Prize in Physiology or Medicine in 1945. Fleming and Florey would both go on to be knighted.

The wonder drug that saves millions of lives around the world each year is today faced with new challenges. It was as early as the late 1940s that reports started to come in of microbes that had become resistant to its effects. Today, so-called superbugs such as MRSA are proving very difficult to counteract. The work of modifying penicillin (and other antibiotics) continues apace in a grim game of catch-up.

The very mould that Fleming found that day in 1928 still exists, on account of the fact that he took the trouble to put it in a glass frame and label it. It was sold at auction in London in March 2017 for £24,375. Meanwhile, the open window at St Mary's through which the mould blithely sailed one September day is commemorated by a purple plaque two storeys below.

No one remembers to steep some strips of gauze in alum water

A classic example of the limits of free speech is that no one has the right to shout 'Fire!' in a packed theatre if there is no fire. The sad truth is that history is littered with instances in which people in theatres have actually had every reason to cry just that.

Shakespeare's Globe was famously lost in a conflagration in 1613, although thankfully there were no casualties. In the 19th century, Glasgow lost no fewer than four Theatre Royals to fire. Exeter, too, was a city where going to see a play was more dangerous than it should have been. One theatre succumbed to flames in 1820, another in 1885. This latter was replaced by the Theatre Royal, which opened in October of the following year at the corner of Longbrook Street and New North Road. This new playhouse had been designed by Charles Phipps, a renowned architect who had been responsible for more than 40 theatres, so hopes were high that it would not meet the same fate as its predecessors.

Monday 5 September 1887 saw the opening night of *Romany Rye*, a romantic play by George R. Sims. No one knows exactly how many people were in to see it that evening, but estimates range between 800 and 900, the initial audience swelled by poorer theatre-goers who bought cheaper tickets that permitted them to watch the latter stages of the performance.

The trouble started at around 10.10P.M., during the fourth act. *Romany Rye* was a play that required a good many changes of backdrop. Three flymen, so called because they clambered about up in the flies (the space above the stage), were responsible for raising and lowering the painted canvases for each new scene. The illumination that enabled them to perform this task was provided by gaslight.

The flymen became confused about which backdrop they should lower for a particular scene. As they were struggling to rectify the situation, they realised that one of the backdrops had caught fire. They cut the ropes on the flaming canvas, in the belief that by dropping it to the stage a hose could be brought on to douse the blaze without further ado. It nearly struck the one actor on stage, a Mr Mouillot, who had been in the invidious position of having to ad lib all alone while the crowds before him grew restless. With the burning backdrop now in a crumpled heap on the stage, the curtain was closed. Although iron safety curtains had started to be used in some theatres, Charles Phipps had not considered that one was necessary for the Theatre Royal.

The fire could have been contained on the stage and the looming disaster averted but for the fact that there wasn't a hose to hand, or a hydrant. Indeed, there was not even a water bucket. Mouillot is said to have cried out, 'For heavens' sake, keep cool!' but with nothing to fight the fire, any cool heads that might have been kept counted for nothing. Even when the stage manager did manage to bring a hose to the scene, no water came out of it.

With flammable material all around the burning backdrop, the fire took hold with frightening speed and within three minutes it was out of control. The audience, however, was still unaware of what was happening, beyond the fact that something had gone wrong with the play – the unfortunate Mr Mouillot's pained improvisations and the impromptu dropping of the curtain were evidence of that.

A Colonel Freemantle, who was watching from the stalls, declared afterwards that the curtain blew outwards as a result of someone having opened a door backstage, giving the audience its first terrifying view of the blaze. The rush of air through the door also fanned the flames, taking them beyond the stage and into the auditorium. Immediately, panic ensued. Shouts of 'Fire!' competed with screams and cries for help as a stampede towards the exits began.

Those seated in the stalls, the dress circle, the boxes and the pit were able to get out of the theatre with relative ease. However, those in the cheaper seats of the upper circle and the gallery – who between them may have numbered between 300 and 400 – were obliged to use a single exit. It was this group who provided the vast majority of casualties.

A broadsheet published by H. P. Such of London the following day carries a reasonably accurate report of the disaster, including the terrible scenes that occurred in the auditorium:

> Flames shot up through the roof over the stage and dense smoke poured forth from every window...
>
> It is almost needless to say that the utmost panic prevailed throughout the theatre, and the terror and bewilderment was intensified a hundredfold at those points where egress seemed impossible. To gain anything like a fair conception of the dreadful struggle for life which took place in the gallery, one has to picture a panic-stricken throng of men, women, and children pushing or forcibly impelled towards the single doorway – the only exit the gallery seemed to have – and followed by the tongues of flame, momentarily increasing until at last the outer fringe of the mass was overtaken by it...
>
> As for those who escaped from this furnace they did so either over the bodies of their more unfortunate companions or through the windows. When the latter alternative was adopted the jumpers often flew from one death to another almost equally horrible whilst others sustained fractures to their limbs. The great mass of men, women and children in the gallery were, however, wedged into an almost immovable mass and the advancing flames roasted them to death...

Soon after the outbreak the City Fire Brigade were on the spot, but the water they poured on the fire was absolutely without effect.

As poignantly captured in *Trapped*, Martin Sorrell's radio play about the catastrophe, there were many heroes and heroines that night, some of whom lost their lives while saving others. The lion-hearts included a Mr and Mrs Thorne, who helped pull two women out through a lavatory window and onto a parapet from where they were eventually saved when a ladder was put up to them. Mary-Anne Dyke ushered groups of theatre-goers out through an exit and managed to open the gate to the pit which, if closed, would have trapped scores of people. Passerby William Tremaine, a 19-year-old artilleryman, rushed into the theatre several times to rescue those inside who had fallen unconscious. The young bombardier Francis Scattergood showed extraordinary courage. Time and again he braved the flames to haul bodies from the theatre in the hope that some might still be brought back from unconsciousness. He failed to emerge from his final foray into the inferno and was in turn saved by able seaman William Hunt, who found him lying unconscious on the floor inside. Hunt saved a good many others that night, climbing repeatedly up a pillar at the entrance to enter the theatre. Curiously, he was unable to repeat this feat of gymnastics when asked to do so in the days after the fire. Sadly, Scattergood died on his way to hospital.

An inquest into the disaster opened the following morning, presided over by the city coroner. It found that the fire had started because one of the calico mediums – blue, red and yellow strips of gauze about two feet wide that determined the colour of the light thrown onto the stage – had been set alight by a naked flame from the gas lamp it was masking. In those theatres where they were still used, calico mediums were soaked in alum water. This is a solution of sodium (or potassium or ammonium) aluminium sulphate that was customarily used to prevent the mediums from catching light. No one had remembered to carry out this procedure during the preparations for the opening night at the Theatre Royal, making a fire almost inevitable.

The coroner's court also found that the theatre was a veritable tinderbox. Not only were laths and match-boarding used in places where their use was expressly prohibited by fire regulations, the building was also lit throughout by gas and candles rather than by electricity. Compounding this, the height of the ceiling above the gallery – just six feet – meant that any smoke would quickly fill the space and choke anyone unfortunate enough to be in it. If this were not enough, there was just one stairway out of the gallery, and the exit door that led to it opened inwards. There had been plans for a second stairway that would have passed through a shop below and out to the street, but this would have meant forgoing the rent from the shop, so it was never built.

The proceedings unearthed a catalogue of deficiencies in the safety measures at the theatre, for which the architect Charles Phipps, the owners of the theatre, the city surveyor and the Exeter magistrates who had been responsible for granting a licence to the theatre were clearly at fault to varying degrees. However, the jury returned a verdict of accidental death on the 186 victims of the fire (a figure that is likely to be an under-estimate). The foreman of the jury added that the magistrates should be censured for their lack of care in ensuring that the theatre was in a fit state to open its doors to the public, and the theatre-owners were at fault for installing an unauthorised pillar and a ticket box, both of which hampered egress from the theatre.

In terms of loss of life, the Royal Theatre fire was Exeter's worst ever peacetime disaster and Britain's worst ever theatre fire. Nearly 100 children lost one or both parents, and many were consequently shipped off to orphanages (Exeter having none of its own).

Although the fire was not the only calamity that took place in Britain around that time, it was one that caused a particular horror among the population – even Queen Victoria sent money to the disaster fund for the victims – and was instrumental in forcing the government into action.

The catastrophe led to the setting up of council-funded fire brigades up and down the country. These replaced the private companies who had, up until then, provided fire services in a much more patchy manner and were often wholly inadequate when faced with major blazes. The Exeter Fire Brigade was established in March 1888. The city was also handed its first electricity-generating station, with the result that the next Theatre Royal to be built was not lit by gas but by much safer electricity.

Legislation was introduced in 1890 that considerably toughened up safety measures in theatres and other places of public entertainment. Henceforth, all theatres were compelled to install a safety curtain and mark their exit doors clearly. Even half a century after the event, the Home Office manual on 'Safety Requirements in Theatres and Other Places of Public Entertainment' cited the Theatre Royal disaster as being one from which lessons had been learnt.

Back in October 1886, the theatre's lessee, Mr Sidney Herberte-Basing, wrote a piece of doggerel which he recited at its inauguration. It included the lines: 'If there be faults, and faults there are no doubt/We'll rectify them as we find them out.' Had he been as good as his word, particularly when it came to the slapdash procedures that led to the carelessness over the calico mediums, those 186 lives would not have been extinguished. The only consolation granted to those who lost loved ones that night was that the legislation brought in after the fire would doubtless go on to save many more lives than that.

Index

Acknowledgements

Books are rarely written in isolation and this one is no exception. I'd therefore like to take this opportunity to thank Elisabeth Whitebread, Rosalind Loten and Stephen Tomkins for their helpful suggestions. I'm particularly grateful to Onor Crummay for giving up her time to pass on some very helpful advice.

I'd also like to record my appreciation to the ever efficient staff at the British Library for furnishing me with vast mountains of books.

I'm keen to express my thanks to my excellent agent Michael Alcock of Johnson & Alcock.

My deep gratitude goes to my editor at Quadrille, Céline Hughes.

And finally, thank you to *you* if you've bought this book, or borrowed it from a library – your taste is, as ever, impeccable.